WAGNER

By the same author
NIETZSCHE

Wagner

MICHAEL TANNER

PRINCETON UNIVERSITY PRESS
Princeton, New Jersey

Library of Congress Cataloging-in-Publication Data

Tanner, Michael.
    Wagner / Michael Tanner.
        p.   cm.
    Includes bibliographical references and index.
    ISBN 0-691-01162-1 (cloth : alk. paper)
    1. Wagner, Richard, 1813–1883—Criticism and interpretation.
I. Title.
ML410.W13T36   1996
782. 1'092—dc20   96-22020

For
Elisabeth Furtwängler

CONTENTS

PREFACE
AND ACKNOWLEDGEMENTS

This book is intended for people who have some, not necessarily very much, acquaintance with Wagner's operas and who feel that they raise questions which are both urgent and difficult. The sensuous appeal of Wagner's art is very powerful, but it also, and oddly, seems to be highly intellectual. And, as reading anything about Wagner soon reveals, it gives rise to a great deal of polemic, much of it soon taking one away from the works themselves and onto the personality that created them, and to broad cultural issues. For an artist who has been dead for more than a century, Wagner's position is uniquely unstable. I want to investigate why that should be so, to put the central points in the arguments as forcefully as I can, and while not disguising the fact that I am a passionate admirer of his work, to see why so many people who are musically and culturally quite catholic in their tastes find his art repellent.

There are no musical technicalities in this book, which means that it is not an explanation of how Wagner gains his effects, but rather an exploration of what they are. Nor have I given plot summaries of the music dramas, since they are available in many books (*see Select Bibliography*), and in the booklets which accompany most recordings of the works.

I have discussed Wagner with countless people over a period of more than forty years. Many of those discussions have no doubt contributed to the views which I now have about his work. But the only acknowledgements which need to be made are to my friend Brian Jones, who encouraged me at a crucial stage of writing this book, and discussed its shape, and many specific points, at a length which amazed us both, but which was unquestionably beneficial. I owe him an incalculable debt; and to Frank Kermode, who asked me to write the book, and was most encouraging and patient about it. The same applies to Stuart Proffitt, who showed in extreme measure the mixture of forbearance and keenness to see the finished item which one hopes for from a publisher.

Michael Tanner
Cambridge, August 1995

1

The Case of Wagner

What is it about Richard Wagner that makes him, 112 years after his death, still so violently controversial? The easy answer would be 'Everything', but it would not be quite right. For no one – no serious musician – any longer doubts that his place among the most significant composers is now secure. That, at least, is a comparatively recent development. Until after the Second World War, which certainly did his reputation no good, and for which, to read some contemporary commentators, one might think he was in large measure responsible, there were still important figures on the musical scene who were prepared confidently to dismiss him out of hand.

But one would be hard put to it now to find that attitude. It becomes increasingly difficult to write off someone whose works remain enormously popular all over the world, whole cycles of the *Ring*, however outlandish the production and mediocre the musical execution, being invariably sold out in advance; and much more so now than half a century ago. Among the musical avant-garde his fate has been more complex: after a period in which many of them, Stravinsky being their leading spokesman (but even he finally recanted), regarded him as a tiresome perversion in the history of music, they have increasingly tended to find him a cause of extreme fascination, and even of inspiration. That has been especially true of the aggressive modernists of the post-World War II era, Boulez and Stockhausen. The latter is still in the process of writing a vast cycle of operas which he knows will routinely be dubbed Wagnerian, on account of their scope, ambition and pretensions. Boulez has devoted lengthy periods of an exceptionally varied and trend-setting career to conducting Wagner, and to writing about him in favourable terms, though his writings seem to urge on us the strange request that we, at long last, come to view Wagner 'objectively'. But how can we, and how can anyone, imagine that we ever will?

We have the phrase 'to put someone in perspective', and we use it in an odd way. For since it has become fashionable, at any rate in philosophical circles, to use the term 'perspectivism', and rather less fashionable to have much of an idea of what that term might mean, people have begun to deny, on what sound like fresh grounds, the possibility of objective truth. And yet when they talk of putting Wagner, or for that matter anyone else, in perspective, they seem to mean getting an accurate idea of him as opposed to being infatuated with or violently contemptuous of him. But there is, if one understands what a perspective is, no such thing as getting someone, and *a fortiori* not Wagner, into *it*. There is only the possibility of taking various perspectives, and seeing how he looks from *them*. What, I think, is meant is achieving a desirable distance from Wagner, being locked in neither embrace nor combat. But what is that distance, and how would we know that we had achieved it? We are back already, too soon, at objectivity, with its connotations of lack of involvement, a capacity for seeing something – Wagner's works, or the whole gigantic phenomenon of works together with life together with influence of many kinds – without taking sides, though we may pass judgement, of a desirably impersonal kind.

A short book which began with a long consideration of

methodology might be tiresome, so I shall take as a kind of motto some sentences from Hans Keller's book *Criticism*:

> But ever since the age of objectivity started, primarily in reaction to so-called romantic hero-worship, this new danger has, as a temptation, presented itself to the evaluating, the *critical* historian – to canalise his own destructiveness into a professional virtue and, inspired by the spirit of detachment, find fault especially where impeccability used to reign.
>
> In the entire history of the Western mind, one chief villain has emerged in the age of objectivity, for a variety of reasons, all of them easy to uncover – RICHARD WAGNER.
>
> (*Criticism*, p. 95)

That does seem undeniable, though I'm not sure about the ease with which all the reasons for Wagner's status can be uncovered. As Keller goes on to say, even lovers of Wagner's music are often haters of Wagner the man, some of them plainly finding something exciting about the contrast in their feelings. And haters of the music often claim that it was written by the kind of person you would expect, granted what it is they hate about it. Music critics, and perhaps opera critics in particular, as we shall see, tend to be naive about the relationship between composers and their art. And even if they aren't in general, when it comes to Wagner the tendency to infer objectionable features in the work from (alleged) detestable personal characteristics proves too strong to withstand, for anyone who dislikes the works in the first place.

Hans Keller goes on to offer his own diagnosis of anti-Wagnerism. But while he makes many shrewd points, it seems to me that he doesn't get to the heart of the matter. His chief claim is that we have a dread of greatness, that the 'age of

objectivity', about which he is efficiently scathing, has super-
vened on an age of hero-worship, which we now view with
embarrassment and distaste. While it is not uncommon to
find a need to cut geniuses, especially self-conscious ones,
down to size, that doesn't provide a sufficient explanation of
anti-Wagnerism, since there are other geniuses whom almost
everyone rejoices in celebrating. Mozart is an obvious case,
even now that the myth of his childlike unawareness of his
gifts has been pretty comprehensively blown. And though
Beethoven is a more controversial figure, I think that that is
not on account of his insistence on the respect due to his
genius.

The fact is that people would forgive Wagner his alleged
megalomania, his genuine anti-Semitism, his (ludicrously
exaggerated) womanising, his conversion from left revolutionary to right nationalist, and anything else known or suspected
about him, if they didn't find something in his music-dramas,
perhaps more specifically in his music, which led them to
reinforce their hostility by grasping at anything about him
that might justify their Miss Prism-style moralising. And
though the hostility, or the expression of it, often takes forms
so shockingly crude that one is tempted to ignore it, it is
important to recognise that its roots are deep. Too deep, it
seems, for exploration by those who indulge – still – in hysteri-
cal denunciation.

Hans Keller has an explanation, one which has been adumbrated by other favourably disposed writers, for this too:

> Wagner's music [Keller was only interested in the
> dramas to the extent that they enabled Wagner to
> express his supreme musical gifts], like none other before
> or after him, let what Freud called the dynamic uncon-
> scious, normally inaccessible, erupt with a clarity and

indeed seductiveness which will always be likely to arouse as much resistance (to the listener's own unconscious) as its sheer power creates enthusiasm.

The trouble with that highly plausible-sounding suggestion is that no one has succeeded in developing it any further, no doubt because to do so would involve independent research of a kind that musicologists are unwilling or unable to undertake; and because, as usual with explanations which derive from Freud, it is hard to know how to set about verifying or falsifying them, even in rough outline. Is the suggestion that those of us who respond passionately to Wagner in a favourable way are unusually well-balanced, or exceptionally neurotic? And that those who find his music repulsive are repressed or threatened by what it audaciously succeeds in exposing?

It seems that the argument could go either way. It is satisfying to Wagnerians to feel that they can cope with uniquely explicit revelations of the contents of their unconscious, and it is satisfying to anti-Wagnerians to feel that they are rejecting the glorification of barbaric forces. This argument, like all serious argument about Wagner, had already been launched by Nietzsche, who, I think it is interesting and relevant to note in this crucial matter, is not illuminating, at any rate in any direct way, in his early pro-Wagnerian writings, but who becomes hugely instructive in his late expressions of fear and loathing. Without having available the resources of Freudian terminology and what it denotes, he had made a claim which can very easily be translated into psychoanalytic terms. It was a general claim about art, which received, he thought, spectacular justification from studying the rampant Wagnerism by which he felt himself to be surrounded, and which not long before he had fervently endorsed.

The claim is that, for the healthy person, art serves to express his sense of over-abundance, extreme vitality, everything to which Nietzsche opposed 'decadence'. By contrast, for the decadent himself – Wagner being the arch-example – art expresses need, lack, an urgent demand and supply in one, making up in fantasy for what is missing in reality. The claim applies equally to the artist and to his audience. It is, quite evidently, questionable in the most straightforward sense, and all the more so because it is so central a claim about civilisation, society, and the various forms which they take. So the Keller-claim that Wagner has a uniquely direct line to the 'dynamic unconscious', and is therefore, though a deeply disturbing artist, also a very great one, had been pre-stated by Nietzsche to Wagner's disadvantage. Wagner gets to the places which no other artist does, but for the Wagnerian that is felt as a liberating, exhilarating experience: Where id was, ego is, when one is listening to *Tristan und Isolde*, say, and it is *Tristan* which is always the touchstone for Nietzsche. But the anti-Wagnerian of Nietzsche's outlook can only lament the neurotic state which *Tristan* appears to cure, and the embracing of the art which deals with it successfully, or seems to. For the Nietzsche of the late phase art which treats illness is itself sick, and there is no hope for those who need it. Art is, Nietzsche had come to think, either celebration of health or comfort for the ailing. It no longer possesses the truth-value which it had done for him in his heady days as a Wagnerian: that he should ever have thought such a thing shows what a plight he had been in. Art is no vehicle of truth, though it may be highly symptomatic, and so inadvertently give away a lot. Whatever one can deduce from art, it is not a revelation of a reality apart from the artist and his audience, as it had been in *The Birth of Tragedy*. Because it is now, for Nietzsche, nothing but an experience *sui generis*, it is impossible to live by it. That is the hideous mistake the Wagnerian makes, and can hardly fail to in succumbing to those hypnotic, narcotic works. As for living, Wagner does that for the Wagnerian; but the anti-Wagnerian does it for himself, or at any rate makes a spirited attempt.

This is still speculative, nebulously so. Yet it would be less than honest for people on either side to deny that something, maybe a large element, in their responses to Wagner is touched by it; at least on repeatedly interrogating my own feelings about him I conclude that it is a line worth pressing on with. The difficulty is that, as in any matter which goes so deep, it ramifies so extensively that it is hard to deal with without also articulating one's reactions to a large number of the most basic issues. All to the good, in one way. But the problem now becomes that while for the Wagnerian it is an excellent and enjoyable thing to be able to focus his attitudes towards many of his central preoccupations by further experiences of Wagner's art, and reflection on them, for the anti-Wagnerian it is painful, or worse still, merely boring, not stimulating, to be led to define his positions by reference to a phenomenon which he finds so cosmically nasty and tiresome. So confrontation at this profound level, which could be most worthwhile, because most searching, tends not to occur. Instead there is endless bickering about aspects of Wagner and his art which is interesting, possibly, but serves to disguise the real conflicts which should be explored, and so the whole discussion is superficial, if impassioned.

It would be different if Wagner were only an artist, whatever exactly that means; or if he had been clearly in the first place something else – a philosopher of culture, or some kind of prophetic figure. But he was, and remains, a musical dramatist trailing clouds of doctrine, and thus a 'phenomenon'. In the former case, he could be just ignored as not to the taste of many ardent lovers of music and drama; in the latter, attacked

7

or ridiculed for the falsity or absurdity of his views. It is the cunning interpenetration of his art and his prosily expressed *Weltanschauung* which makes him unavoidable, together with his immense influence in so many disparate spheres. No wonder that those who resist take refuge in unrestrained polemic – they want to obliterate him, so that he can simply cease to exist as the object of endless discussion. But their polemics only fuel counterblasts, and achieve just the opposite effect from the 'marginalising' which they had hoped for. In his own last, splenetic writings on Wagner, Nietzsche acknowledged that too. There is, and will remain, a 'case of Wagner' so long as we are stuck in the cultural crisis which Nietzsche diagnosed, because Wagner embodies it to an extent which no other artist approaches.

The issue is complicated by a further one which makes Wagner's music-dramas very different from almost everything else in the operatic tradition, Schoenberg being the only notable exception. Wagner was intensely concerned that we should feel rather than think in the presence of his works. Here at least his hope has been fulfilled. But for many people, whom for convenience's sake we may call Brechtians, that in itself renders him suspect. However, it is worth noticing that they attack Wagner not so much for saying that he wanted emotional rather than cognitive responses to his art, but for the works themselves, which seem to demand an incessantly high-level emotional response more insistently than any others. But the Brechtians don't attack Verdi, for instance, in the same way, or so far as I know at all, despite the fact that his operas provide stimulus for feeling rather than thought – indeed the idea of thinking in relation to Verdi is odd. Who could reflect for long, and relevantly, on *Il Trovatore*, a masterpiece of its kind, but one which can only excite and move us in presenting with such vigour a succession of situations each of which is stirring? Wagner is the most intellectual of musical dramatists (Schoenberg again excepted, and up to a point Pfitzner in his explicitly Wagnerian masterpiece *Palestrina*); not by dint of the prodigious theoretical writings and continuous musings, in correspondence and conversation, about everything under the sun, if not indeed the sun itself; but by virtue of the subject-matter of his works and the kinds of issue which his characters are involved in and are articulate about. Sometimes in Wagner's works it seems as if he were setting philosophical dialogues to music, the victory being awarded not to the character who argues most convincingly, but to the one who, to put it not quite accurately, has the best tunes.

In fact one can say that Wagner would not have been so insistent that we should respond by feeling rather than by thinking if he hadn't realised the extraordinarily dense quality of the thinking which is going on in both the words and the actions of his dramas. The relationship between thought, or 'reason' or 'intellect' (the German word is '*Verstand*') as Wagner more often puts it, and feeling, was something which he wasn't so inclined to be simple-minded about as what I have thus far said suggests. He devotes a long section of his major theoretical work, *Opera and Drama*, to the subject, and produces many penetrating and novel formulations, of which perhaps the most subtle can be illustrated by this quotation:

Nothing should remain for the synthesising intellect to do in the face of a performance of a dramatic work of art; everything presented in it must be so conclusive that our feeling about it is brought to rest; for in the bringing to rest of this feeling, after its highest arousal in sympathy with it, lies that very peace which leads us to the instinctive understanding of life. In drama we must become *knowers* through *feeling*.

9

As so often with Wagner's formulation, one could wish that he had expressed himself a little more clearly, at the same time as one sees what he means, and is impressed. He felt the truth of what he wrote here so powerfully that he made it, in slightly adapted form, part of the actual subject-matter of his last drama, *Parsifal*. And in fact the feeling which the sympathetic spectator or listener has, in the face of Wagner's works, is remarkably accurately caught by it. They do typically work at an extremely high emotional pitch, which is resolved in the final minutes of the dramas. Therein lies much of their enormous appeal, expressed as succinctly as possible in Wagner's statement of his purpose just quoted. But the progression of feeling which they induce is also precisely what makes them suspect for many people. For it involves a huge measure of trust in the artist, the more so when he pitches things at so intense a level. As we are swept through his works, mesmerised through the means which Wagner to a unique extent commands, critical distance is made impossible (so the argument goes), and we could be persuaded by him of *anything*.

It is interesting that this passage from *Opera and Drama* is quoted by Deryck Cooke, one of Wagner's most ardent intelligent admirers, at the beginning of his vast, regrettably unfinished study of the *Ring*, entitled *I Saw the World End* (the rather strange title is taken from some discarded lines which were at one stage part of Brünnhilde's peroration in *Götterdämmerung*). Anyone who writes at length expounding the significance of Wagner's works has, it would seem, to ignore this claim. Cooke's position is that it holds good for the dramas apart from the *Ring*: 'with the others, we do find that our feeling is set at rest, that nothing remains for the intellect to search for, that our instinctive knowledge of life is enriched, and that we become "knowers through feeling"', he writes. But he thinks that things are different with the *Ring*, and that therefore a commentary of great thoroughness is required in order to make its meaning clear. But that suggests, surely, that the *Ring* is some kind of failure.

It seems strange of Cooke to make this distinction between the other dramas and the *Ring*. All of Wagner's works require exegesis, not because they are flawed or opaque, but because even if they do in some way enable or help us to become 'knowers through feeling', the 'synthesising intellect' still has an enormous amount of work to do, and of a highly profitable and strenuous kind. The question is what it has to get to work on; and the answer is the feelings which the dramas have aroused in us, even if they have, in the closing sequences, been in some sense set to rest. For clearly it is possible for music, with its phenomenal resources of creating harmony and order out of their opposites, to persuade us that a dramatic resolution has been achieved. One of the reasons why there are so few operatic tragedies is that composers have been tempted, and have nearly always succumbed to the temptation, to show that however desperate things get dramatically, it is never beyond the powers of music to rescue them. That makes operatic criticism a very tricky business, since the critic can't ignore the music, obviously, but has to decide on the exact role which it has been called upon to play.

The easy way out, where Wagner is concerned, is the one which Nietzsche finally took, and Adorno after him, in his polemic *In Search of Wagner*. Both writers point to the pervasive idiom of Wagner's music, and ask, rhetorically, whether you think that you can trust a man who employs those means in order to get his message across; as one might point to a politician and ask why someone who meant what he said and had something worth saying should indulge in that particular mode of speech. They have every right, indeed duty, to ask the question, but not to make it into a rhetorical one – the asking of rhetorical questions being itself an activity which needs scrutinising. Wagner is, *par excellence*, an artist who has designs on us, and who therefore leads us to examine anew the Keatsian view, winning because of the very innocence of its dogmatism, that we should mistrust all such artists. The innocence – one which is shared by both Nietzsche and Adorno, but they go to inordinate lengths to establish their sophistication – is in imagining that there is any art which does not have designs on us, palpable or otherwise. No doubt we want, in the presence of art, to feel a peculiar freedom, and the more so the less we feel it elsewhere. That was Kant's claim: that the autonomy of the aesthetic artefact has a close relationship to the autonomy of the spectator (auditor, etc.), indeed makes it possible as it is not anywhere else in our lives, where we are ruled either by the laws of Nature, non-prescriptive but nonetheless ineluctable; or the laws of Morality, easily violated but peremptory and absolute (to use George Eliot's intimidating formulation). But whatever the content of 'freedom' in our responses to art, it seems that the more palpable the designs an artist has on us, the freer in one way we are, since there is then no question of our thinking that he is merely presenting us with 'the facts' if he is making it perfectly clear what attitude he wants us to adopt to them.

When we are dealing with a mixed art-form, such as opera, not to speak of the *Gesamtkunstwerk*, a kind of art which combines all the other forms, which is what Wagner wanted his mature works to be, the question evidently becomes more complex still. If we divide opera into action (or plot), text and music, then the crucial issue is the role that music plays. In his most famous dictum, Wagner claimed that in traditional opera music, which should be the means, had become the end, while drama, which should be the end, was merely the means. His revolution in opera, as opposed to all the other revolutions which he hoped to effect, was to be the placing of music and drama in the right order. To establish from first principles what that order was, Wagner was driven to his heroic amount of theorising, much of it unacceptable because it is so vague and groundlessly speculative. But what we can certainly agree with is that however much music is in the service of drama, it has, in the hands of all the operatic composers whose work survives, a capacity to direct our sympathies which none of them has failed to exploit. It may well be that opera is all the more effective when that is not what it appears to be doing, but that is chiefly to say that we admire the cunning of self-concealing enterprise.

It can seem that Wagner refuses to join in the time-honoured procedures of the artist, that he manifests in his dramas the lack of tact which was so striking a feature of his personality in general, and that his reverence for Beethoven is most apparent in his taking over the insistent nature of Beethoven's music, a source of pain to his most fastidious listeners. We shall have to see about that. But it is an impression which many people have gained from listening, in the first place, to highlights from his works, the usual way, perhaps, of hearing things by him. Which brings me to the topic which someone who hasn't yet seriously encountered Wagner's art, but is thinking of doing so, is likely to be preoccupied by.

2

Prejudices and Banalities

What I would like to do now is move immediately to a consideration of key aspects of Wagner's work, by discussing some of his dramas and the themes with which they are concerned. But at some point I have to deal with an enormous amount of controversy that still rages about many aspects of his life and personality, and which, if one ignores it, is brought up as something which renders pointless any other discussion. Of course one can't hope to transcend the controversy: Olympian postures in relation to it merely fuel it further. Nor, given the questions around which it revolves, can one hope to settle it. The only course is to wade in and make, as succinctly as possible, what one regards as the crucial points, emerging on the other side in as decorous a state as one can contrive.

It is presumably some evidence of what is taken to be a strikingly direct mode of statement in Wagner's works which leads people to feel that the alleged facts of his life are relevant to understanding and judging them in a way that doesn't occur elsewhere in music, music-drama, or literature – and this in the case of a dramatist whose sympathies might be expected to be distributed among his characters. There wouldn't be a 'case of Wagner' if he had not been one of the most significant figures in the development of music and opera. But if he had led a life of sufficient ordinariness for his biography to be a bore, the case of Wagner would be much less insistent and incessant than it is.

A few recent examples, to show the level to which one has to descend if one is not to be felt to be just *con*descending. In his strikingly intelligent and serious *A Guide to Opera Recordings* (Oxford University Press, 1987), Ethan Mordden writes: '*Parsifal* is a lie, for Wagner was a sinner: hypocrite, bigot, opportunist, adulterer' (p. 170). That telling 'for' could only have been used on the assumption that *Parsifal* is meant to be a proclamation of belief, and that if someone doesn't behave in the way which he is taken to be recommending, he is a hypocrite. There are many disputable remarks in Mordden's book, but this is the only one that seems to be evidently inane. Only about Wagner would anyone venture to make it.

In *The Times* of 15 February 1993, Rodney Milnes, one of the most earnest of opera reviewers, wrote apropos of *Tristan und Isolde*: 'Nearly six hours spent in the theatre being button-holed with long-winded and specious justification of the composer's taste for other people's wives in general and Mathilde Wesendonck in particular is wearing on one's patience.' So that's what *Tristan* is! Probably Milnes would claim that he was only high-spiritedly letting off steam, taunting those members of the audience who might be taking the work too seriously: '*Tristan und Isolde*, an obsessively morbid and unhealthy work . . .' the paragraph containing the previous quotation begins. But why the rage, why the dragging in of Wagner's private life (actually a grotesque version of it)?

In *The Times* of 13 July 1993, another critic, Barry Millington, one of the leading 'experts' on Wagner of the present time, acclaimed a production of *Die Meistersinger von Nürnberg* for revealing 'the dark underside of the opera'. 'In short,' Millington writes, 'the opera is the artistic counterpart of the ideological crusade launched by Wagner in the 1860s: a crusade to urge Germany to awaken, to expel alien elements and honour the "German spirit". The characterisation of

Beckmesser is demonstrably anti-Semitic.' The 'demonstration' which is supposed to support that adverb is contained in an article by Barry Millington, published in the most self-consciously high-brow of contemporary opera journals, *Cambridge Opera Journal*. Clearly the tone is a more solemn one than Milnes's, but that shouldn't conceal the crass confidence with which Millington presents as fact his own preposterous opinions. To demonstrate their absurdity would be out of place here; I will merely point out that to the extent that the article in the learned journal claims to make its point, it is by the accumulation of a large number of clues which no one has ever picked up on before, and that by its very ingenuity it refutes itself: Wagner was often subtle, but he didn't write in code. It might have occurred to Millington alias Holmes that Wagner, in the cause of his crusade, should have rendered his message to the German nation somewhat more accessible.

To grasp fully what leads people to write about Wagner in this way – and every reader will agree that there is no other major artist who elicits remarks of this kind, as methodologically absurd as they are deliberately provocative – we shall have to wait until examining some of Wagner's art in some detail. But we don't need to wait until then before acknowledging the strangeness of the hostility, its intensity and its reaching for any weapon that comes to hand (minds hardly seem to be involved) to clobber Wagner with. The most obvious feature of all the remarks quoted, and one that pervades anti-Wagnerian polemic, is the simplicity of the transition from features of Wagner's extra-musical activities to animadversions on his art. One doesn't need to have been involved in the intricacies of the dispute about the 'Intentional Fallacy', the tersest statement of which was 'the design or intention of the author is neither available nor desirable as a standard for judging the success of a work of literary art', to feel that the relationship between an artist's life, including his intentions in producing his art, and his actual artistic productions, must be a matter of some complexity. Yet though this is widely accepted for virtually every other case in the history of art, it is utterly ignored when we come to Wagner. This would be, perhaps, understandable if he had been a villain on a prodigious scale (some people think that he was). But adulterers, hypocrites, opportunists, even anti-Semites, are not all that uncommon in the artistic community or outside it. Wagner never behaved with such extravagant malignity as Beethoven, for example, in relation to his sister-in-law, or so dishonestly as Beethoven to his publishers. But though Beethoven's biographers tend to deplore his irrational behaviour, amounting sometimes to insanity, they, and other people, never, so far as I know, find that a reason for questioning the greatness of *Fidelio* or the Missa Solemnis or the Ninth Symphony. And those who are favourably impressed by Peter Shaffer's portrayal of Mozart in *Amadeus* tend, like its author, to find an extra frisson in celebrating the achievements of so otherwise comprehensively idiotic a figure as that play depicts, not to feel that they are diminished.

So is it simply that there is something uniquely *unattractive* about Wagner's character, which puts him in a category by himself? And what kind of thing is it? As I quoted Hans Keller saying, people do find his consciousness of his own genius distasteful. The reiterated charges about his emotional, libidinal life seem absurd, since he was not promiscuous on a particularly large scale, or as much as many artists, and others, who have been are accorded forgiveness by their virtuous commentators. But there is the impression that his various unattractive facets somehow – no one has said exactly how – add up to, are part of, an integrated character which is, again *somehow* congruent with his music, or the dramas of which it is a crucial part. It is thought to be, especially by those who have heard little of it, overbearing, noisily emphatic, erotically charged even in the most inappropriate passages, and effusive in a way that leads to suspicions about its sincerity.

But then why not just write it off? When one contemplates the immense annual production of anti-Wagnerian propaganda, the suspicion becomes inescapable that for many listeners his art presents a threat, if not a temptation. Among other things, to admire it seems to be committing oneself to allowing him to take up more emotional space than one artist, or at least one artist who practises his peculiar forms of persuasion, should be allowed to do. A striking moralism comes into play in his case, as it rarely does elsewhere. Perhaps the fundamental anti-Wagnerian argument can be fairly presented in these terms: even though he is writing dramas, Wagner himself is omnipresent in them, in a way that Shakespeare impressively is not in his dramas, or even Racine in his. So the total effect of any of them, at any rate the mature ones, is of coming into contact with a personality all the more powerful for dispersing himself into all his characters. And such is the force of his art that he turns his listeners/spectators into accomplices. Becoming a Wagnerian is, at least incipiently, becoming like Wagner. That was, once again, Nietzsche's claim.

But why becoming like Wagner, as opposed to becoming like what Wagner presented himself as, granted that one accepts the argument at all? For the difference seems to be immense. The staple of Wagnerian drama, the whole idiom, is one of nobility.

All the worse, the reply comes back; by a variety of means Wagner conveys the impression of an earnest orator. But what he really is is a brilliant demagogue, whose rhetoric is so resourceful that we naturally find it suspect. Anyone who genuinely believes what he says – this is our prejudice, unexamined and even sacrosanct – can communicate it without going into constant overdrive. Nietzsche, the incomparable and tireless exposer of our prejudices in all fields, subscribed uncritically to this one. Contrasting Mozart and Wagner, he cleverly takes the music that Mozart gives the Commendatore when he appears in the Supper Scene of *Don Giovanni*, a passage of most atypical violence and emphasis, and writes: 'Apparently you think that *all* music is like the music of the "Stone Guest" – *all* music must leap out of the wall and shake the listener to his very intestines. Only then you consider music "effective". But on *whom* are such effects achieved? On those whom a *noble* artist should never impress: on the mass, on the immature, on the blasé, on the sick, on the idiots, on *Wagnerians*!' (*Nietzsche contra Wagner*). Once more, as so often with Nietzsche's sweeping charges, this contains illuminating truth as well as outrageously unfair falsehood. But it does rely on the view that the genuineness of a conviction can be assessed by its mode of communication, and that the extreme nature of Wagner's art, *'espressivo* at all costs', as Nietzsche puts it elsewhere, betrays an uncertainty. Either that, or it hides something. Wagner's surface of nobility conceals his underlying insecurity and egoism, not to mention his pusillanimity.

It is almost impossible to find out whether these things would be said about Wagner if his well-advertised personality defects weren't known about, because the advertisement has been so successful that no one has escaped hearing about it. Even people who take no interest in music can retail odd facts about Wagner. So I shall now do two things, for the rest of this chapter: first, consider some aspects of Wagner's life and character. Secondly, see to what extent his alleged views and vices are thought to be evident, in more or less indirect ways, in his work. There is, to begin with, his overbearing personality and strength of will, remarked on by everyone who knew him, and one of the most powerful sources of his fascination for them. This urge to dominate, combined with a charm which he could exercise whenever he felt inclined, and which he is claimed to have used to manipulate people with the sole aim of furthering his own ends, was realised by many of those in thrall to him, and even accounted for their willingness to serve him until, as with Nietzsche, they revolted against such tyranny. But some who had problems reconciling their own need to create with moving in Wagner's orbit found that it was, in the end, possible to do both, and a risk worth taking. Peter Cornelius, composer of the winning comic opera *The Barber of Baghdad* for instance, broke with Wagner and then went back to him. He wrote to his future wife: 'I am quite determined to stick to him steadfastly, to go with him through thick and thin, partisan to the last ditch. When I see how others, like Bülow, Liszt, Berlioz, Tausig, Damrosch treat me, ignore me, forget me, and how he, the moment I show him even a hint of my heart, is always ready to give me his full friendship, then I tell myself that it is Fate that has brought us together.'

Next, there is Wagner's financial history, a spectacular affair, certainly. From an early age he was in debt, chronically so, partly because he rarely had a settled source of income, partly because he never ceased to indulge his love of luxury, one of the traits which earned him most ridicule as well as disapproval from his contemporaries, as one can see in many cartoons. Anyone who lent him money, and most of the people who came into contact with him did, was foolish to expect that they would ever see it again.

His treatment of the women who played so large and indispensable a part in his life is also a subject of self-righteous recrimination. Once more, it may not be the sheer number that were involved, but rather the ruthlessness with which, if they had more than a one-night stand with him, they tended to get treated. This is supposedly true of his first wife, Minna, to the most extreme degree, but of at least half a dozen others too.

Last, most serious and now most often used as conclusive evidence against him, there is his racism, of which the two correlative elements were an ever more virulent anti-Semitism and an insistence on the necessity of the purity of Aryan blood if mankind was not to degenerate (a concept that was becoming very fashionable towards the end of Wagner's life) to a point where it was irredeemable.

The strength of will and ruthlessness in pursuit of his aims is something we may freely grant. The question, insofar as it concerns a moral judgement on Wagner's character, is whether it was exercised only for his own gratification, or whether it was of the kind which anyone with a serious and radical programme of reform of what they regard as vitally important is bound to employ. Whatever one thinks of Wagner's attitudes, artistic and socio-political, he was an idealist. He was by no means bent only on the furtherance of his own fame, glory, and so on. He was, to a remarkable degree for a revolutionary artist, a hero-worshipper of his greatest predecessors. During the period of his life when he did have one job, as director of Dresden's musical life, from 1843 to 1849, he raised standards of musical, especially operatic, performance and production to a level which had not previously been envisaged. In order to get for Gluck the recognition which Wagner felt he deserved and lacked then (as to some extent now), he not only gave what seem to have been exemplary performances of his works, but in the case of *Iphigénie en Aulide*, which he felt was flawed in ways that obscured its merits, he extensively rewrote it. A misconceived enterprise, it might be thought. But it was carried through without thought of his own interests, and at the expense of his own creative work, for which he had far too little time, since his administration of the opera house was so conscientious. These things need bearing in mind. For what we routinely find in scholarly works is this kind of claim: 'Wagner's monomania is well known. In his whole life there seem to have been hardly any occasions when he was capable of disinterested co-operation' (M. S. Silk and J. P. Stern: *Nietzsche on Tragedy*, p. 216). The authors proceed to cite a rare exception; but note the shape of the argument. They don't need to give any evidence for Wagner's monomania, since it is 'well known'. So the counter-example *must* be an exception. It is in that way that myths become history.

What galls people even more than Wagner's idealism is that he was a *practical* idealist. He succeeded in making real what his contemporaries regarded as ludicrous pipe-dreams. But many of them were in the interests not only of great art, with which his only connection was passionate devotion, but in the interests of those who were performing it. He had a lifelong concern with the welfare of the musicians with whom he performed, and who idolised him. He drew up detailed and carefully worked-out plans for the betterment of the Dresden orchestra, and did a great deal to put the careers of the musicians in Zurich, when he was exiled there, on a secure financial footing. He believed, from extensive experience, that they were unlikely otherwise to give of their best, but there is no reason to think that that was his only or primary motive; unless one is determined to see him as 'an absolute shit' and 'a very bad hat indeed', to invoke two of W. H. Auden's judgements on his character.

Wagner's preparedness to be as hard on other people, in the fulfilment of what he saw as his mission, as he invariably was on himself, is undeniable. And it is easy to slide from that to his 'using' people. The prize example here is King Ludwig II, and it is worth looking at his relationship with Wagner in a bit of detail because it is so common to regard the King as the pathetic but rich host, Wagner as the impoverished but triumphant parasite. In the most famous single episode of his life, Wagner, in 1864, was in hiding from his creditors, at the end of his financial and all other tethers, when the eighteen-year-old Crown Prince came to the Bavarian throne, and as his first act sent his cabinet secretary in search of the composer whom he had idolised since early adolescence. Having finally run Wagner to ground, the secretary Pfistermeister conveyed his royal master's greetings, Wagner went off to Munich the next day, and Ludwig promised to settle all his debts, set him up in the comfort he needed for completing the *Ring*, and ensure its production. A Platonic honeymoon ensued, but was short-lived. The populace of Munich was scandalised by Wagner's behaviour, he made enemies in the cabinet by attempting to influence Ludwig's political opinions, and later on he lied to him about whether he was having an affair with Cosima, the wife of Hans von Bülow, the conductor who was tirelessly preparing the first performance of *Tristan und Isolde*. Their relationship continued until Wagner's death, but Ludwig was, for all his passion for Wagner's art (more its scenic than its musical aspects), sadly disillusioned with its creator, whom he once included in a denunciation of 'the theatre rabble'.

It is, in many respects, a painful story. But the truth is that Ludwig, in his lonely misery, found his chief consolation in watching Wagner's dramas. He wanted them finished and performed for himself alone – his preferred way of seeing them was in a theatre in which he constituted the sole audience. He was one of the first of the breed of people who have found

Wagner's dramas superior to life, and in straightforward competition with it, and was unusual among them only in that he had the means at his disposal to build himself a Venus Grotto, a Hunding's Hut (both in the grounds of his pleasure palace Lindenhof), and to spend a large part of the time which should have been occupied in affairs of state pretending to be Lohengrin. There is no single piece of evidence that he wanted 'to save Wagner for the world', as he put it on hearing of Wagner's death, to which his immediate reaction was, 'Oh! I'm sorry, but then again not really. Only recently he caused me trouble over *Parsifal*.' And as for the expense which Wagner caused him – and it does seem very unlikely that without Ludwig's aid Wagner's later works could have been written – the decorations for Ludwig's bedroom in Herrenchiemsee, his recreation of Versailles, cost considerably more than all the money and gifts in kind that he gave Wagner over nineteen years; and his wedding coach, never used, three times as much as he gave Wagner. The treatment he received from the composer was compounded of genuine gratitude, warm affection and concern at the start, and exploitation in the service of his art.

Admittedly Wagner wrote in a letter to Liszt: 'If I am obliged to plunge once more into the waves of an artist's imagination in order to find satisfaction in an imaginary world, I must at least help out my imagination and find means of encouraging my imaginative faculties. So I cannot live like a dog, I cannot sleep on straw and drink common gin: mine is an intensely irritable, acute and hugely voracious, yet uncommonly tender and delicate sensuality which, one way or another, must be flattered if I am to accomplish the cruelly difficult task of creating in my mind a non-existent world.' That does strike me as candid. If, on the basis of it, hostile judgement of Wagner is in place, he would even so not be worse than many people who escape the criticism that is heaped on him because he told the truth and was incessantly in the limelight; quite apart from the reputation he has earned from producing his works under the conditions, some of the time, which he tells Liszt he craves. Quite a lot of the time he managed to create them despite poverty and discomfort, but I don't see that he should have had to endure more of that than he did. All told, I'm inclined to feel that Wagner's capacity for making writers on him, many of them securely established in academic jobs, reveal their priggish and disapproving lack of imagination is his most vexing feature.

However, on to Wagner and sex. After some youthful galli-vanting of a commonplace kind, he married a woman who was in no respect suitable for him, and their life together was unhappy for the most part. Very shortly after the marriage his wife Minna ran away with another man, twice. Her sexual history had begun distressingly, with a seduction which led to the birth of a daughter, Nathalie, whom Minna always passed off as her sister, and thanks to Wagner's loyalty, the secret was not discovered during her lifetime. Minna was a great admirer of Wagner's worst work, *Rienzi*, and was unable to understand why he felt the need to write operas vastly different from it, which were less successful at the box office and led to lengthy periods of near-destitution. That they didn't give up the effort to live together until decades of misery had passed is a mystery. Under the circumstances, Wagner's intermittent passions – he always needed a muse – are in no wise surprising. And what was certainly the grand passion of his life, for Mathilde Wesendonck, though it caused all the parties con-cerned great pain, was hardly anyone's fault. Its connections with *Tristan* – was Wagner in love with Mathilde because he was writing *Tristan*, was it the other way round, or a mixture of the two? – can never be sorted out, if only for the reason that this is one of those matters in which there is no such thing as the truth.

His second marriage was as mutually fulfilling as his first was frustrating. Cosima, illegitimate daughter of Liszt, had married early in her first attempt at self-sacrifice to a man of genius, Hans von Bülow. Unfortunately he was tormented by not being genius enough, and their marriage was, in its way, as unhappy as Wagner's first. Since for Cosima, a woman of extraordinary gifts, it was inconceivable that she should not play the part of a George Eliot heroine to someone who needed her, it was inevitable that frequent contact with Wagner should lead to passion. As so often in such situations, the idea was that in concealing their relationship from Bülow they would spare his feelings, though of course that is never possible. Cosima's guilt over the deception pervades her diaries, written after everything was in the open. She and Wagner would have been fools to refuse to enter into what became one of the most famously productive partnerships in history, Cosima giving him every kind of support, except financial, during the last eighteen years of his life when he was bearing crushing burdens of responsibility, creative and otherwise, and his health was in decline. Wagner had one last fling, with Judith Gauthier, in the period of the first Bayreuth Festival, an affair of which the remarkable Cosima was aware and which she sanctioned, knowing that it would not survive for long.

So if Wagner had 'a passion for other men's wives', as the familiar account goes, that may be due to the fact that most women he met were married, a problem he wouldn't encounter now. He certainly didn't welcome the complications that they involved. Once more, I find it hard to understand the fuss.

But it is all too easy to understand the fuss about Wagner's anti-Semitism, which was virulent even for the time, and moved from what seems to have been a mildly paranoiac state to one of obsession. That he was in the company of many of the most distinguished men of the day makes things no better, though racial theories are not evidently absurd, indeed the reverse. Wagner suffered from a lifelong need to locate the evils of life and society in one area, and it is not surprising that, in carrying through this boring programme, he should have selected the Jews. He was no more anti-Semitic than, say, Luther or Kant or Marx, but he was nearer in time, except for Marx, to the vilest of all racially-based political programmes and its enactment. And since the Nazis were so violently anti-Bolshevik, that has let Marx off the hook.

To say that many of Wagner's best friends were Jews may sound like a weary defence, but it is not meant as a defence at all, merely as a sign that his attitudes towards Jews were inconsistent. The crucial question is whether his anti-Semitism invades his works. If it does, then they are even more controversial than they have always seemed, and in a way that is bound to take them finally beyond controversy into repugnance – except for those who thrill to the unsavoury. Though it is a crucial question, I believe it can be rapidly answered, as I indicated at the beginning of the chapter in mentioning Millington. If they are in any respect anti-Semitic, then that element in them is coded. They are, that is, to be sharply distinguished from *The Merchant of Venice*. But Wagner was the most explicit of men, both in the whole of his tactless life and in what is often thought to be his no less tactless art. Where are the Jews in his works, and how are we to recognise them? The chief focus, until recently, for Jew-spotting has been the *Ring*, since it is allegedly about the evil of possessions. That leads many commentators to claim that Alberich is a Jew, and even more obviously Mime. But if they are, so is the whole race of the Nibelungs, and they are depicted as pathetically downtrodden workers, the very image of the misery for which Jewish capitalism is responsible. Apart from which, Alberich is not as simple a villain in the *Ring* as casual acquaintance with it might lead one to think. He exists in intimate relationship to Wotan, who is referred to as 'Licht-Alberich' (Light-Alberich). The plot of the *Ring* simply can't be worked out in racial terms. And the fact that Wagner devoted many pages in his letters to expounding its meaning, and that Cosima's *Diaries* are full of references to it, without the question of its Jewish 'sub-text' ever cropping up, surely is decisive.

More recently – and it is interesting that it is after the Nazi period that most of this discussion has taken place, not during it, even on the part of the Nazis themselves, who would have been keenest on Jew-spotting – it has been alleged that some of Wagner's other major villains are Jewish, for instance Beckmesser in *Die Meistersinger* and Klingsor in *Parsifal*. Once more, why did Wagner make the point so obscurely that we have had to wait more than a century for these 'discoveries' to be made? The very elaborateness, for all its fatuities, of Millington's argument for Beckmesser's Jewishness is a refutation of the claim.

But how, one might wonder, could anyone be as obsessively anti-Semitic as Wagner without its entering his works? One might well wonder, but the gulf between the life and opinions of an artist and his creative work has surely been sufficiently established by now for us to admit that such extraordinary discrepancies are more frequent than the congruities we obstinately continue to expect. If we don't accept that, we are going to lapse into the circularity of claiming that Wagner thought Jews were bad, and so the villains in his works are Jewish; and you can tell how much he disliked Jews from the ghastliness of the bad characters in his works. That is the level of sophistication at which these arguments operate.

That was originally all I was going to say on the subject, since I have already had to repeat myself in order to appear to take the issue seriously. But of course it has to be taken seriously, in some sense. Since I wrote this chapter there have been two books on the subject in English alone, and in a series of programmes on Channel 4 on English television, called 'Wagnermania', it was clear that Wagner's anti-Semitism is the one aspect of him which the series' sponsors felt guaranteed an audience. Not that anything new is forthcoming. In fact, the presenters of the argument that Wagner's works are insidiously anti-Semitic, including the ubiquitous Millington, were at pains to point out that the 'fact' might all too easily be overlooked by audiences, unless they were instructed in what Wagner wrote in his pamphlets, and said to Cosima. The authors of the two books have to adopt a similar line. One might feel, under the circumstances, that it would be better if they kept the information to themselves: not because it damages Wagner, but because it is unclear how informing people that Alberich is 'really' a Jew is giving them anything which serves any purpose in understanding the *Ring*. Supposing that Wagner intended that he should be seen in that way. In the first place, it is only within a certain framework that calling someone a Jew has any significance. It isn't as if the rest of the characters in the *Ring* are threatened Aryans, or uncorrupted until Alberich takes his decisive action. In the second place, the advocates of the final solution to the Wagner problem, as one might call them, are all arguing on the basis of Wagner's alleged influence on the Nazis. It might be thought scandalous to say 'alleged'; but only Hitler was an enthusiastic Wagnerian, insisting that the functionaries of the Third Reich attend performances of the dramas which bored them stiff.

And if Hitler had taken the dramas seriously, he would hardly have felt encouraged to pursue his policies, since Wagner shows the futility of political action in dealing with the world's evils. He might have noticed, too, that the only major character in the *Ring* who survives it is Alberich, and been disheartened.

That there are some similarities between the Nazis' proclaimed ideology and some of the conclusions which Wagner may be suggesting in his dramas – though as we are about to discover, that is no simple matter – I am not disposed to deny. But to attempt to draw any systematic conclusions from that is futile, especially if it is a matter of blaming Wagner for their outlandish views. Oddly, it is widely agreed that there neither was, nor could have been, any great Nazi art. But the people who say that are prepared, nonetheless, to say that there was – *avant la lettre*.

Basta! No one ever changes sides on these issues. I just hope that I have got in first for people who have not yet taken sides, and provided them with some rudimentary equipment.

3

Getting under Way

Having in the first chapter floated a fair number of ideas, and in the second sunk, I hope, several of the most popular misconceptions about Wagner, I can now move on to a discussion of what is in the first place important about him: his musical works, which I shall designate as dramas, music-dramas or operas indifferently. His first artistic impulses were theatrical, music entering at a slightly later stage. Enormously excited as a boy by the sheer atmosphere of the theatre, and then finding the music of, above all, Beethoven deeply moving, it was clear that he would, if he was to be creative, combine thrills and emotions in the most popular contemporary form, that of opera. Contrary to the impression he sometimes gives in his many autobiographical retrospectives, Wagner received a thorough training in the elements of composition, through assiduous study of the masters of counterpoint. When he came, at the age of twenty, to compose his first opera *Die Feen* ('The Fairies'), the chief constraints on what he wrote were those of having no very urgent need to communicate anything. It is very rare in Wagner that we feel a gap between his aspirations and his capacities – but all he aspired to at this stage was to be an opera-composer, with no particular subjects or themes in mind. As an ardent admirer of E. T. A. Hoffmann, and in love with the atmosphere of early German Romanticism, he sedulously devoted himself to producing a work which caught the spirit of Weber as fully as possible. The opening bars of the Overture to *Die Feen*, and much else besides in the work, might have come from Weber working at less than full pressure.

The result is a work of considerable charm, not much originality, and a pervasive uncertainty about how seriously it wants to be taken. One of Wagner's most important statements of his development, *A Communication to my Friends*, written nineteen years later in 1851, makes a good deal of the fact that some of the central themes of his later works are adumbrated in *Die Feen*. Up to a point that is true, but as always the question is at what level they are dealt with, and the level of *Die Feen* is nothing to get worked up about; though it is certainly as enjoyable an opera as many that are revived these days to cries of the thrills of rediscovery. It is rather a long work for its slender substance, but it is at least as well worth hearing as most of Mozart's or Verdi's early operas, to take a couple of cases of severe contemporary overvaluation.

Despite its irrelevance for any serious consideration of Wagner, *Die Feen* is a plausible starting-point for a composer whose preoccupations were later to be with the supernatural, with the centrality of love as leading towards some mode of redemption, and with the expression of his dramatic themes in a German musical idiom. His next opera, *Das Liebesverbot* ('The Ban on Love'), based loosely on *Measure for Measure*, can only be seen as an act of fairly gross infidelity to his muse. True, there are some passages that give a foretaste of Wagner's later works more strongly than anything in *Die Feen*, and the tumescent motif which appears in the Overture, and in the scene between Friedrich (the Angelo figure) and Isabella, is strikingly characteristic. But the whole ambience of the work, its celebration of uninhibited hedonism, is utterly remote from anything that one thinks of as Wagnerian. In fact Wagner was going through a rebellious period, in which 'German' signified for him what it vulgarly does for many people – heaviness, soul-searching, and in musical terms a lack of interest in sustained singable melody. He was infatuated with the music of Bellini, the supreme *bel canto* composer, and a love-worthy object. But although Wagner never lost his affection for Bellini's work. he soon came to realise that he was not destined for that path – or rather, that for all its appeal it wouldn't serve his purposes. And in fact he was only able to use Bellini by misunderstanding him. He even went so far as to write an alternative aria for Oroveso, to be inserted in *Norma*, Bellini's masterpiece. Listening to that aria one is amazed that Wagner thought he had captured the flavour of Bellini.

In *Das Liebesverbot*, which is once more an enjoyable opera, though again somewhat overlong, it is possible to feel that the young Wagner was putting up a misguided battle with his destiny. It manifests, if not with consummate skill, at least with gusto, many of the things which he was to spend the rest of his life fighting against with single-minded dedication. The theme of the ban on love itself he revisited in one work after another, but in his mature output the various ways in which the ban is brought into operation are seen as deep elements of human nature, as the concept of love itself becomes something of increasingly daunting complexity. But in *Das Liebesverbot* the figure of Friedrich, who imposes the ban, is a one-dimensional caricature, and a hypocrite to boot. He merely provides what suspense there is in the plot, while Wagner is mainly keen to express a mood of carnival and enthusiastic youthful rebelliousness. No comparison with the Shakespeare play would have any point: Shakespeare produced a deep, and in my view deeply flawed, work. Wagner produced something which doesn't reach a level where serious criticism is appropriate. He was, as it were, shopping around. His first opera was an attempt in the German mode, reflecting what

Wagner took to be his concerns; his second was one of those trips across the Alps which Goethe seems to have made obligatory for Germans at some stage of their career.

With almost too handy comprehensiveness, Wagner's next effort, *Rienzi*, the last of what have been widely and rightly agreed to be his juvenilia, was an emulation of grand French opera. Though it is artistically the least satisfactory of these three works, it provides more interesting food for thought than do the first two. Wagner tried to produce a grand historical tragedy, basing it on the novel by Bulwer Lytton. On its own terms – or rather those of Meyerbeer, who had set the fashion for this kind of oversized period drama, with its compulsory ballets, spectacular scenery and vast cataclysms – it is successful to a degree that makes one fear for Wagner's integrity at this stage. Perhaps it is fairer to say that since he still lacked an artistic identity, there was nothing to be singleminded about. And yet the beginning of the Overture, the first piece of Wagner's music to have retained its place in the repertoire, is original, moving and unmistakable. It starts with a long-held trumpet note, evocative both of majesty and suspense, and then moves into the first great arch-Wagnerian melody, richly scored for strings. That melody, which provides Rienzi with the material for his Prayer at the beginning of Act V, has a nobility which almost everything else in the work betrays, including most of the rest of the Overture, a blowsy piece which, once it moves into its allegro stride, skirts vulgarity with a Verdian brio, though it is much more heavily scored than anything by the Italian master.

This theme, which can't be called a motif, since it is too fully-formed and monolithic to be plastic enough for that purpose, clearly indicates the hero's greatness of soul. But in the work itself Rienzi has to become a figure who has been forced to sink to the level of the intriguers around him, so that there is a disjunction between his portrayal in the opening section of the Overture and everything that comes later, apart from the recapitulatory prayer. The only way that Wagner can resolve the action is through a suitably apocalyptic conflagration, as the Capitol is ignited by the angry crowd and Rienzi is immolated along with his visions. Once more, if one were so inclined – many commentators are – one could trace connections between elements in *Rienzi* and the later works, including, very obviously, the conflagration at the end of the *Ring*. But such comparisons are more likely to subtract from the sublimity of *Götterdämmerung* than to add to the stature of *Rienzi*. That Wagner was fascinated by certain types, and by what might happen to them, is clear enough. But it is merely confused to think that later versions are nothing more than the earlier ones with sophisticated and far greater music to lend them glamour and plausibility. In the case of many of the greatest artists who can, in a sensible way, be said to have subjects, they show what those subjects are going to be from their earliest works. But what makes them great is their capacity for working with certain terms and endlessly exploring and deepening them, until the connections with what they started out from are better disregarded. Otherwise we get nothing more than an example of the 'fallacy of origins', by which the developed form of something is alleged to be no more than its elementary form cosmeticised.

Unfortunately this tendency is especially pronounced with Wagner's critics, and all the more so since it was attending a performance of *Rienzi* in Linz which set Hitler, so he often claimed, his goal of absolute power. It may have done, though if he fancied himself as a reincarnation of Rienzi he must have paid scant attention to the action. Perhaps this is one thing for which Hitler can be forgiven, since *Rienzi* is written in an idiom which discourages concentration. With its spectacle and its elaborate diversions, it was the ideal work for those who went to the opera for 'effects without causes' – Wagner's cruel and famous characterisation of Meyerbeer's operas, which also applies in large part to *Rienzi*. In fact one wishes that the opening weren't so arresting; it raises expectations and suggests a degree of seriousness which are willingly granted. But when they aren't fulfilled, what may happen is that instead of spending five hours being disappointed, one takes the actuality of the work at a higher value than it deserves, lapsing again into the mistake of thinking there are such things as serious subjects, as opposed to serious treatments of them.

All of Wagner's three early operas are on a virtually unprecedented scale, at any rate in the history of German opera. He indulged himself in them, letting an impressively far-ranging imagination have its head, at the same time that he was developing his capacity for thinking in long time-scales. Their organisation is rudimentary, but they must have given him confidence in his ability not to let things simply get out of hand. Prentice-work though they are, and worth only occasional airings, they would have established him as a composer of unusual ambitions. But the work which, even if Wagner had never written another, would have remained permanently among the great operas, was his next and most evidently concise drama, and the one in which, at one bound, he found himself – by no means all of himself, but what he did find was wholly genuine and strikingly deep. There may be no other example of a composer so suddenly moving from competence in various idioms of his day to commanding mastery which was partly rooted in tradition, but equally impressive for its necessary departures from it.

The famous opening of *Der fliegende Holländer* has the hallmarks of all Wagner's openings from now on: it compels attention, and lets one know instantly what the matter in hand is. Viewed with hindsight, it achieves other ends too. It sounds not only as if Wagner is making a declaration of having found his real self as a composer, but is also showing how he relates to the most admired figures and works in the tradition from which he emerges. For the raging first pages are in D minor, the demonic key of Mozart and Beethoven. *Don Giovanni* opens in it, and equally cataclysmically. No other operatic overture before *Holländer* begins so arrestingly, and with music that is part of the fabric of the main action. And Beethoven's Ninth Symphony, a talismanic work for Wagner, and one which he had made a piano arrangement of when he was seventeen, has given nineteenth-century music its definitive D minor statement. Though Beethoven begins almost inaudibly, while Wagner's Overture rages, they are both elemental, and both use the same material and some of the same devices. Wagner, as always, has his roots in the physical, even though his ultimate intentions are metaphysical; Beethoven evokes a primeval chaos which has no truck with physicality. It would be pointless to press the similarities, but if they were not conscious, that is all the more striking. At any rate, the demands Wagner is going to make on us are clear, and they are immense.

But it is not the Overture that I want to dwell on, rather the drama it portends: for, quite apart from the elemental sweep of *Holländer*, it is a simple, but certainly a serious treatment of a subject which is at the top of Wagner's agenda throughout the whole *oeuvre*, and so, besides its intrinsic compellingness, it is a valuable way into his world, as the three works which precede it are not.

The story is familiar. The Flying Dutchman, whose story Wagner took from Heine, but without the irony – Wagner is the least ironic of artists, at least within his individual works: the ironies exist in their relationship to one another – is, in crude outline, the prototype of the Wagnerian protagonist:

someone who has done something so terrible that he has to spend the rest of his existence looking for salvation, or redemption, which comes only through the agency of another human being, even when, as in Wagner's first three and last dramas, there is a certain amount of theological background (usually vague and non-specific). Though it is characteristic of Wagner's central figures that they have committed a crime – in the Dutchman's case, an oath that he would round the Cape at any cost, for which Satan doomed him to eternal voyaging; in Tannhäuser's that of sojourning with Venus; in Wotan's that of making a bargain which he has no intention of keeping – it seems that really Wagner was a Schopenhauerian from the start. He only read Schopenhauer in 1854, instantly becoming a disciple.

Schopenhauer claims that living itself is the original sin. That Wagner always held a position which amounts to that comes out in the fact that the 'redeemers' in his works long to redeem just as much as the sinners long to be redeemed. Hence it is entirely appropriate, and could well have been a planned effect, unquestionably casting light back over a lifetime's work, that the final words of *Parsifal*, intoned by the chorus, are 'Erlösung dem Erlöser' ('Redemption to the redeemer'). Taken by themselves, or just in the context of *Parsifal*, they are a riddle. But it may not be too difficult to solve it if one surveys the series of characters, often though not always female, who do the redeeming. In *Der fliegende Holländer* Senta needs the Dutchman quite as badly as he needs her. Her life is without a genuine purpose, it only has a visionary one until he appears on the scene. The various ways in which the sinner/redeemer relationship is worked through is among the great fascinating topics for meditating on Wagner's works – and one that, in the notoriously vast 'literature' on them, is weirdly neglected.

So the Dutchman himself, given a teasing chance every seven years of setting foot on land to find a woman who will sacrifice herself for him, begins the Duet with Senta, which is the heart of the work, with an unaccompanied solo which is more groan than song, and more interiorised recitative than melody. But it does move, gradually, into song, quietly punctuated by the orchestra, as he feels the faintest stirrings of hope, exhaustion hardly daring to give place to a new attempt at salvation. Then, to tense tremolandi from the strings, he moves into a statement of what he feels, which is expressed by a slowly rising melodic line and then a declamatory mode which hovers between song and enhanced speech. The words:

> Die düstre Glut, die hier ich fühle brennen,
> Sollt' ich Unseliger die Liebe nennen?
> Ach nein! Die Sehnsucht ist es nach dem Heil,
> Würd' es durch solchen Engel mir zuteil!

> (The sombre glow that I feel burning here,
> Should I, wretched one, call it love?
> Ah no! It is the longing for salvation,
> might it come to me through such an angel!)

In his justly famous essay 'Sorrows and Grandeur of Richard Wagner', Thomas Mann quotes these lines and rightly comments, 'never before had such complex thoughts, such convoluted emotions been sung or put into singable form'. And he adds, 'What a penetrating insight into the depths of an emotion!' (*Thomas Mann Pro and Contra Wagner*, p. 95). But in his account of *what* it is that the Dutchman is discovering himself to be feeling, Mann seems to me to go astray. For he takes it that the Dutchman is in love with Senta, whereas it is a case of his mis-identifying, and then correctly re-identifying, a feeling. Just as Wagner is, according to Nietzsche's sneer, always thinking about redemption, so he is always meditating on love. And since the soaring last melody to be heard in the *Ring*, often taken to be its final 'message', has routinely been miscalled 'Redemption through Love' by the commentators – an error which Wagner himself corrected, via Cosima – it is easy to conclude that his preoccupation is, if not always, then very often with how love might redeem.

But that is to assume that Wagner has a fixed idea of what love and redemption are, and is concerned with the mechanism by which the former effects the latter. Whereas his works constitute, along with a great deal else, a sustained investigation, often amounting to downright critique, of what love may be, and of what it is we seek when we seek redemption. He inherited an extremely well-worn vocabulary, which embodies the conflicting valuations of two millennia of Western civilisation; and thus he found himself in a profound predicament. Either, because his views were so radical and disruptive, he could coin a new vocabulary, but one which we wouldn't understand, or would rapidly assimilate to the old one. Or he could use the familiar terms, with all their ambiguities and conflicting forces, and see how they could be put to new but indispensable work, thanks partly to the dramas in which they are saliently employed, and partly to the effects of the music, itself an integral part of the drama.

At no point in his life, so far as I am aware, did he put his problem and his mission in such bald terms, though he might (could) have done. For he was a slow developer, and what he achieved was an ever-increasing complexity of thought and feeling on these matters. *That* was something he was certainly aware of; and his endless retrospectives, autobiographical writings, reinterpretations of his life and art, are to be judged in large part not as being historically accurate – their failings in that respect have been at least sufficiently castigated – but as attempts to make sense of the process of making sense itself. His is a curious case, possibly a unique one, of an extraordinarily articulate artist who simultaneously mistrusted his own fluency. Hence his compulsive need to go on talking and writing. He viewed his works with a mixture of proud possessiveness and bemusement. And in some cases he not only gave conflicting accounts of what they meant, but remained dissatisfied with the works themselves. *Tannhäuser*, which he rightly felt to be unsatisfactory but too good to write off – it was also highly popular with his contemporaries – was something that, a few weeks before his death, he told Cosima 'he still owed the world'.

But more often than revisions after the deed, he went in for, or found himself involved in, lengthy gestations. It has often been noted that halfway through his life Wagner had drawn up the agenda for his artistic productivity for the second half, as well as planning several major works which he never executed, and would not have done, though he sometimes wrote the complete text. Evidently he could not have considered someone else as a librettist. He sometimes said of his works that he had written the text and now all that remained to be done was to set it to music, and commentators with less perceptiveness than they need have taken it that the music was being composed in his head as he wrote the dramas. But that is absurd on many counts – not least because there was often a long interval between the writing of the text and the musical composition. And as a composer Wagner developed, between his first works and his last, at least as much as any composer ever has. In his writings he was as concerned to redeem his music-dramas as in his music-dramas he was concerned to redeem his characters (most of them, anyway). Because he was always occupied with certain very general issues, he was insistent on his works as constituting a genuine *oeuvre*. If it is not the case, as it is with Nietzsche, that each of his works left him with issues unresolved which demanded the composition of a further one, it is still true that their interrelationships are vital to understanding them, and that characters in one reappear, almost, with a different name, in another. Discretion has to be exercised in pursuing this line of thought – and, as we shall see, wasn't always by Wagner himself.

To return to the Dutchman and the passage that I consider so crucial: the duet in which it occurs is hardly a 'love-duet'. Actually Wagner didn't compose nearly as many of those as he is often taken to have done. Certainly the movement is one of powerfully operating mutual magnetism, but the magnetism is not of an erotic kind – not quite. Erik, Senta's unlucky suitor, and Daland, her father, naturally take it to be. But they show, by doing so, how much they belong to the world of marriages and children, both of which are, in nearly all cases, comically irrelevant to Wagner's predestined pairs. One of the things that annoys people about Wagner is that his 'lovers' seem to be more interested in verbal, albeit sung, communication than in getting on with consummating their relationship. Very often, though not, as I said, in *Holländer*, there is a strong erotic charge in Wagner's music that would seem to indicate that a sexual act is imminent, or is even being performed, but in musical code. He is, in fact, the composer who can write the sexiest music of anyone, though he is rarely capable of the come-hither, seductive (in the strictest sense) kind that comes so easily to Mozart, in Susanna's 'Deh vieni, non tardar' or Don Giovanni's duet with Zerlina 'La ci darem la mano'. His most famous 'seduction scene' is in *Parsifal*, indeed constitutes most of the Second Act, and Kundry still fails. The only one that succeeds is Gutrune's of Siegfried in

Act I of *Götterdämmerung*, and that is affected by an aphrodisiac with amnesiac properties. Wagner is not interested in the mechanics of seduction as such; he is concerned with the forces which bring people together, and which are out of the control of either of them.

That is clearly the case in the Duet in *Holländer*. Senta has long been familiar with the portrait of the Dutchman which hangs in the spinning-room. It represents for her an idea which becomes her ideal: self-sacrifice for an endlessly tormented man, something she gives alarming voice to in her breakaway in the middle of the third stanza of her Ballad. Like Tamino in *Die Zauberflöte*, she had her imagination ignited by a likeness. Wagner is already intimating that what comes first is the need, focused on a representation which reality obliges by copying. The relationship Senta wants has already been worked out before she sets eyes on the person who incarnates it. It is a theme which will recur in *Lohengrin*, in the *Ring*, in *Tristan* and in *Die Meistersinger*. Love in Wagner so often occurs at first sight because it has already begun in, as it were, second sight.

That leads to a further crux in reactions towards Wagner. His characters often lead listeners to feel ill at ease because they appear to embrace impossibly elevated notions of self-sacrifice, while at the same time the same characters seem to be abnormally, even abhorrently, self-obsessed – a reflection, the conclusion is often drawn, of their composer's highly ambiguous state of mind. How is it possible to give, Derrida has been asking recently, in the context of a circle of exchange which turns the gift into a debt to be returned? But that is only putting into a specific context a question which is raised whenever the subject of selfishness and selflessness is considered. Wagner's 'givers', redeemers, are, as I have remarked, no less desperate for someone to redeem than the converse.

And this appears to have the consequence that his characters don't relate to one another so much as relating to an idea of one another, which reality more or less obliges with. Thus both Senta and the Dutchman begin their Duet in reverie, Senta just as self-absorbed as he is. Whereas he misidentifies his yearning for redemption as love, for a moment, she wonders what she should call 'the pains within my breast', which are, she concludes, a longing to save him. Like Beethoven's Leonore, with whom Senta shares several salient features, she is less interested in the identity of the man whom she sees before her than in what she can do for him. 'Wer du auch seist' ('Whoever you are') she sings, using precisely the words that Leonore uses in the dungeon-duet in *Fidelio*, at which point Beethoven's music undergoes a marked intensification. Senta pretends that she will marry him because she will always obey her father – the Dutchman has asked her, after their rapt individual musings, whether she approves her father's choice – and the music comes down with a rude thump, momentarily, to Daland's level, before the Dutchman makes her an offer, or rather asks her a question, to which she can hardly say no. And then he, like Florestan in his prison cell, having a vision of Leonore as an angel leading him to salvation, tells her that she is an angel.

There are one or two awkwardnesses in this prototypically Wagnerian duet: the cadenza which the soloists indulge in is a non-contributory throwback; and the drop into mundanity, though it makes a point, makes it a bit too baldly. But the overall structure is maintained with moving mastery, and Wagner already shows how he can take us through a huge process of feeling in a comparatively short time without giving any sense of a hectic comic strip, as Verdi so often embarrassingly does. And the Duet does comprehend all the relevant aspects of the work: the Dutchman's tiny burgeoning hope,

Senta's lonely need, the distance – this is a particularly impressive stroke – between the pair at the beginning, even though they are dwelling on the same theme. Then, to electrifying effect, the entry, for the first time in the Duet, of the Dutchman's motif of ceaseless wandering, a compressed account for Senta's benefit of what he has to endure and what she will have to share if she doesn't have 'ew'ge Treu' (eternal fidelity). Once that has been made clear, Senta is free to express with full, explicit conviction that she knows her 'sacred duty', and they surge together to the close, when Daland re-enters bumptiously.

No one, in music-drama or elsewhere, had achieved an effect like this before. It is not, perhaps, surprising that it still remains unclear to many listeners what the effect is, apart from the overpowering sense of two figures being drawn together by a force which lies deeper than any kind of attraction that they feel for one another. The cunning proportions of music, and sentiment, which differentiate them and those which they share give us an uneasy feeling that there is a degree of manipulation which Wagner contrives to present as inevitability. And the manipulation is one which – if it exists – is exercised on the listener as well as on Senta and the Dutchman. It is the more disturbing because it brings into question the nature of quasi-erotic feelings. Already, at this almost alarmingly early stage in his career, Wagner shows himself to be a master of a certain kind of effect, which will grow immeasurably in intensity and profundity in his later works, but which is already sufficiently complex for us to sense a dominating presence demanding submission. For people who find it understandably questionable, as Nietzsche came to do to a degree which necessitated the pretence of wholesale rejection, it is (this is only a first, tentative formulation) as if the drama which Wagner created is one in which the dramatist's will is imposed on the characters, and in turn their ecstasies are transmitted to us, so that the circle is closed and we are, as it might be felt, engulfed in Wagner's feelings. He seems to deprive us of the possibility of achieving a perspective on the drama, which means that in a sense it is *not* a drama. For the genuine dramatic experience, as we have come to understand it, is one in which, however intense the actions on the stage, however sympathetic some of the characters may be and however revolted we are by others, we are still witnesses to a whole process which leaves us with the freedom to judge and assess. What Wagner seems to do – not always, but often enough for it to be fairly called characteristic of him – is to present us with a set of data which are, as it might be put, the premisses of the drama, and which often involve, it is soon made clear, portentous issues on which we are to ponder as well as about which we are to have feelings. But as he proceeds, the movement of the drama leads us to make exclusions which egg us on to identification with the figure, or often the pair of figures, whose supreme intensities of feeling over everything else that is happening lead us to respond so intensely ourselves that any question of checks or balances is eliminated. It is like, or it is, brilliant hypnotic rhetoric in action which disguises, by a remarkable combination of blatancy and subtlety, its ineluctable movement towards a clinching climax which – and it is no good postponing the word indefinitely when discussing Wagner – intoxicates us. The immediate effect is of an undreamt-of expansion of consciousness, giving us an intimation of a level of living which perhaps only Wagner can communicate to us, but does communicate so forcefully that we are led to think we can make it our own. The longer-term effect is of a closing down of alternatives, so that we seem to be left with the brutal imperative: Either live like this or you aren't living at all. But we can't by ourselves live on such exalted terms; we don't have, in Erich Heller's phrase, such 'resources of ecstasy'. So the upshot is that we become addicted to the only art which does that for us: we become Wagnerians, dependent on the magic brew of an astonishingly persuasive mixture of something like sex and religion, a transcendence of the ordinary conditions of life which is, as many have remarked, the prolonged artistic equivalent of an orgasm.

That is the case for the prosecution, put as cogently as I, not believing in it, can manage. I shall not try to refute it directly, but rather take aspects of Wagner's works, the ones which I think are most relevant, and see how far they are adequately accounted for by such an accusing account. If the account – the accusation – itself is something of a hotchpotch, that is not only fair to the level of critique to which Wagner is subjected (when it is trying its best not to be merely abusive), but also a faithful report of the confusion which Wagner generates in the minds of his audiences.

4

Domesticating Wagner

Anyone who has a passing acquaintance with *Der fliegende Holländer* might feel that I have been making heavy weather of it, or around it, though heavy weather is a large part of its subject. Surely, it will be argued, it is at most a fine example of early German Romantic opera, a stirring story set to frequently exciting music, but not to be singled out from other more or less equally successful examples of the genre, such as Weber's *Der Freischütz*, another story of a demonically driven man and a loving, self-sacrificing maiden. But admirable as *Der Freischütz* is, it belongs firmly in the realm of the folk opera, and its atmosphere is that of the Grimms. Probably it is impossible to carry out the thought-experiment of viewing *Holländer* without taking into account Wagner's subsequent spectacular development. But to the extent that I am able to, I still find the stupendous surge and toss of the Overture evokes metaphysical as well as physical vistas. Though he is an incomparable nature-painter in music, Wagner's interest in it is always sentimental in Schiller's sense: there is no nature-evocation in his works which does not affect, and reflect, moods of the human beings who exist in it. Even his most famous portrayal of a natural process, that of the Rhine flowing at the beginning of the *Ring*, is potent with hyper-natural associations. For before the Rhine gets properly under way, there are those famous bars scored for the lowest strings and wind at the bottom of their registers, more sound than music, which are wholly static, and suggest that we are being taken back to the beginning of all things. As Wagner told Liszt in a famous letter, the *Ring* depicts the beginning and end of a world, including the beginning from which the world in which it takes place evolves. Once more one thinks, as Wagner surely did, of the opening of Beethoven's Ninth Symphony. Wagner loves and is awed by Nature, its wildness and majesty, but he invariably anthropomorphises it at the same time.

However, the Wagner of *Holländer*, enormously in Beethoven's and Weber's debt, was still, many people feel, obviously an apprentice. Up to a point they are right. I am not claiming that Wagner, in one mighty bound, arrived at a maturity of method and message. Nonetheless, although *Holländer* may be fairly taken as an exciting evening in the theatre (or, more likely nowadays, at home), it does announce the terms which Wagner throughout his life would imbue with richer and deeper meaning; and it shows, at the least, his potentiality for depth. It is not surprising that in later life he regarded it as the first of his authentic works. Of course, if you find Wagner's obsessions tiresome because irrelevant, you will appreciate *Holländer* more for its crude freshness, its lack of the extreme emotional temperatures which pervade some of the later works, and are often thought to be omnipresent in them, though that is false.

When an artist returns, in work after work, to the same preoccupations, it is easy for criticism to weigh in and celebrate his progress to maturity, finding his early efforts touching in their simple-minded adumbrations, attentively reading more into them than they can seriously bear. It is also easy to schematise the *oeuvre*, overlooking the variety of new concerns. What it seems almost impossible not to do, perhaps in Wagner's case more than anyone else's, is to postulate a presence which is given the artist's name, and then to indulge in the construction of an artistic biography which runs in parallel with the life the artist actually had. And despite the most solemn methodological pronouncements about the illicitness of inferences from the art-life to the lived one, or vice-versa, it proves, over and over again, irresistible. All the more so when the art is of so compelling a kind, and the life so spectacular. In Wagner's case, once more, the originator of this romantic connecting was Wagner himself. He constructed a life, in his unreliable autobiographical writings and oral reminiscences, which imparts an even more ferocious teleology to the series of works than they manifestly possess. And conversely he justified his existence by the somnambulistic assurance, made all the more glamorous and stupefying through its zigzagging course, with which he brought the works into being. The categories by which the art demands to be judged are taken over from the terms in which Wagner made sense of his wildly implausible existence, one which was an outrage to everyone who, persuaded by this devastating force of will, still failed to succumb to his tirelessly self-justifying rhetoric. His occasional insistences that he viewed his creations with the baffled but tremendously impressed gaze of the outsider, striking as they are, and no doubt sincere, failed to counter the drive towards the celebration of a unique degree of integration, forged from the most disparate and recalcitrant materials.

Why is Wagner so interested in people who have committed a terrible deed, and why should we share his interest? How much moral cum metaphysical baggage does one have to take on board in order to regard his works as more than bizarre actions set to frequently wonderful music, granted that one isn't going to be so lazy as to feel that something important is going on, but that it is better not to try to find out what it is in strenuous detail? It is in a praiseworthy attempt to answer that question that many recent opera producers, or directors as they are increasingly often called, have gone in for highly specific interpretations of his dramas, and though I believe that their efforts are fundamentally misconceived, I find their rationale sufficiently convincing (to other people) for them to merit some consideration. I have in mind primarily the school of directors who emanate from what until six years ago was East Germany, and their epigones.

They operate on the following premises: first, every work of art is anchored in the time and place of its composition, and can only be understood on that basis. Any attempt to render the timeless significance of a work in a production is hopeless, since there is no such thing. Second, Wagner's works in particular need drastic re-presentation, in the first place because they are even now tainted with the Nazi ideology by which the very vagueness of their import rendered them exploitable. Third, because in the first post-war productions of them which had great impact, those of Wieland Wagner, they were freed from their past only to be presented again in terms of their 'purely human' significance, a basic error which Wieland shared with his grandfather. Fourth, since the conditions, economic and therefore political, under which Wagner conceived and wrote his works were sufficiently similar to our own to mean that they can cast light on our situation, so long as they are treated with the proper kind of disrespect which great creations deserve and require, one would only be doing him a favour by eliminating a spurious universality and replacing it with an involving topicality.

Besides these broadly Marxist productions, which are now less likely to be well received than they were a few years ago, there is a wide range of styles which sometimes employ the catch-all title 'post-modern' to cover their nakedness, and which involve a mixture of times, places, and costumes; Wagner's works are not, according to them, to be understood in mythological terms, as he naïvely thought, since the time for mythologies is past. We should draw on psychoanalysis, surrealism, and other twentieth-century movements in the humanities, so that once again we can make of these works what we will, but only within limits. This kind of production – and there are correlative written interpretations – has in common with Marxist ones the premiss that there is no such thing as an unchanging human nature to appeal to, though it isn't clear how that is compatible with using psychoanalytic insights, which were thought, at least by their founder, to have universal application.

What all these contemporary ways of viewing Wagner have in common is a desire to make him smaller, in one obvious way, in order that he will be seen to be relevant, which will in turn render him a service, even if it takes some of us time to realise that. The effort to make him smaller is not, then, necessarily a manifestation of hostility to him and his works; rather hostility to Wagnerism. Up to a point it parallels something which we are becoming very familiar with in 'Shakespeare studies', and also in many productions of Shakespeare, though he doesn't have the accumulated bad reputation of Wagner to be cleared of. The idea of 'alternative', 'political', etc. Shakespeares is to question his time-transcending genius, in the interests of genuinely responding to him. It is no paradox, we may warmly agree, to say that we might learn much more from Shakespeare if we ceased to deify him, as both directors and critics have pointed out, while they engaged in their apparently ungrateful task, in both senses of that word. We – those of us unfortunate enough to have received a traditional humane education – have been brought up to revere Shakespeare (while admitting that like everyone else he occasionally potboiled) in a way that removes the possibility of entertaining questions about the success of some of his master-works. What often happens – and it is an increasingly fashion-able critical move – is that the unease we may feel about *Hamlet*, say, is relocated as an unease the play allegedly feels about itself. Or its subject-matter is changed, in line with feelings about its central characters. *Hamlet* becomes a study of a pathological case, Oedipally-fixated or not, and ceases to be the portrayal of 'the most adorable of heroes', and a great deal more to that effect that was prevalent in the nineteenth-century heyday of Hamlet hero-worship. Or if, as is more plausibly argued, the play exhibits (or attempts to conceal) deep fissures, the plot having been taken over from a traditional revenge-play, while Christian elements are brought into the foreground, then that provides us with a fascinating study of a playwright giving voice to sharply conflicting values within his own culture. Whether the play is a success or not hardly matters: there is, it is implied, something childish about such a preoccupation.

There is a lot that is attractive about such a sophistication of approach, especially if it leads to more intensive study of what actually occurs scene by scene, line by line, in *Hamlet*. But it is noteworthy that it always tends in a similar direction: figures who were automatically described as 'heroes', in the sense both of being the central figure and of having the kind of status that the Greeks ascribed to Achilles, now dissolve, dramatically, into a 'complex of meanings' and simultaneously lose their noble stature. That may not constitute a serious criticism of this approach, but it does indicate that we have a strong need to assert the human all-too-humanness of the figures to whom we were previously keen to allot exalted status. The factors contributing to this change of outlook are bewilderingly numerous and different in kind from one another: acting together they can seem to be devastatingly effective. If Shakespeare is still great, it is not because he is beyond criticism but because he can absorb so much of it, becoming, if anything, much more interesting because so much at odds with himself. And so, in his honesty, he is re-established as great in quite another way from what we used, rather touchingly, to think.

The prognostication for treatment of Wagner along these lines, an activity which has been under way for the last thirty or so years, is considerably more complex. For he is very explicitly concerned with the heroic, with heroes and heroines who will effect a cleansing, transfiguring, redeeming change in the whole world in which they live. If the full-blooded notion of the heroic has to be abandoned, how can the *Ring* above all, but the other dramas too, survive? The question branches into two: in what way can we any longer give sense to the notion of a hero, as relevant to any conditions we might encounter? And what, even if we can, is the mechanism by which a hero has effects on a community which are commensurate with his own private (as it were) stature?

If Wagner's works were merely spoken dramas, they might well have been written off in the face of these questions. But the greatness of his music makes that impossible. That, however, is not the end of the matter, since the music functions in the service of the drama at every moment. So we seem to be in an awkward position: a set of postulates about the possibilities of human nature which many people are unable to accept is set to music of vivifying appropriateness, thereby apparently validating, in the way that music so treacherously can, those unacceptable postulates. It took the arch-iconoclast and *enfant terrible* of the post-war musical scene, Pierre Boulez, to hit on a solution. His most notorious proclamation was that the opera houses of the world should be burned to the ground, but he accepted two invitations to conduct at Bayreuth for several seasons each, and for what seem to many Wagner's most questionable works, in very different ways: *Parsifal* in 1966, the *Ring* in its centenary year, a decade later. The effects were predictably sensational, much more so in the *Ring* than in *Parsifal*. For the latter work he took over Wieland Wagner's magnificent 'timeless' settings and production, which tolerated an indefinite variety of musical renderings without incongruity. But for the *Ring* he was given a free hand in selecting the director, and he chose another *enfant*, in some ways still more *terrible*: Patrice Chéreau. And in one fell swoop the *Ring*, which if it is not Wagner's most sublime achievement is certainly his central one, was domesticated and demythologised, in fact deconstructed. A new era was born, in which Wagner's artistic image was *aufgehoben*, to employ that indispensable German word when dealing with German cultural phenomena: i.e. it was cancelled, transcended and preserved. Wagner, in this self-celebratingly 'unfaithful' French production, was firmly put in his historical place, even if it was rather a vague one – but some time during the last one and a half centuries, give or take the odd anachronistic spear. But since the action can't proceed without them, they are, almost every director has agreed, a wearisome necessity. And if they look odd alongside tuxedos and hydro-electric dams (the Rhine), that adds to the sense of epic theatre. Chéreau's was, broadly speaking, a Marxist *Ring*, much as Shaw had envisaged the work in *The Perfect Wagnerite*, though he might have been surprised, and not favourably, by the production. The gods were humanised with a vengeance, even vengefully. A collapsed crew from the outset, it was hard to see how anyone could give a damn about their *Dämmerung*, or even to see what that could amount to. Fricka's savage argument with Wotan in Act II of *Die Walküre*, to the effect that Siegmund is merely Wotan's pawn, was driven home hard. And in case one might think that Siegfried really did have to go it alone, he was provided with a hi-tech forge in Act I of *Siegfried*, while the dragon in Act II was nothing more than a large toy, amusing and not faintly frightening, with which Siegfried played at fighting. This was also, and significantly, the first *Ring* for our sitting rooms. It was videoed, as every self-respecting and Wagner-mocking production of his operas now is, and it was probably seen by more people, when it was televised, than the *Ring* had been before in the whole previous century of its existence. Domestication, in other words, was as manifest in its mode of transmission as in the nature of the staging. Going with this, and an essential ingredient in its success, was an elimination of any sense of natural beauty – this was the first ecological *Ring*, taking place in an environment industrially polluted beyond hope of return. Was there any hope for the world in this *Ring*? Chéreau responded by putting the question of whether there is any hope for the world in any *Ring*: cloth-capped workers out of Brecht-Weill stared at the audience as the last bars were played, leaving them to meditate – this was, after all, a *Ring* to make us think. There is no evidence yet that it has succeeded.

One might have expected the music to sabotage this reductive localisation of the production, but that would be to reckon without the peculiar gifts of Boulez. If he couldn't actually interfere with the notes of the score, or the text – ludicrously violated by the action, often – he could at least play fast and tight with them. Other conductors have taken Wagner rapidly – possibly Wagner himself, certainly Albert Coates, whose many recordings bear eloquent witness to how well that can be done. Naturally it is not speed alone which determines the weight of a performance. But Boulez combined rapidity with lightness, creating, it was said, chamber-music textures, ensuring that the all-important bass parts were undernourished, and eliminating 'false pathos', i.e. pathos whenever it threatened to intrude. But he and Chéreau cunningly contrived to put maximum emotional stress on particular 'human' moments. Thus, in the terrible scene at the end of Act II of *Die Walküre*, where Wotan has to preside over the death of his own son Siegmund to fulfil his promise to Fricka: in the Chéreau production, instead of Wotan's leaning on his spear and gazing sorrowfully at Siegmund's corpse (Wagner's stage direction), he gathered Siegmund in his arms for a passionate posthumous embrace. It provided an overwhelming moment, certainly. But in its extreme expressiveness, just where Wagner had indicated restraint, it counteracted the intended effect of inexpressible grief. And so throughout the cycle: Wagner's intense musico-dramatic effects were suppressed, his reticences overridden. Boulez, made anxious by, unable to cope with, top-level rhetoric, got it over with as soon as he could. Thanks to Chéreau's extraordinary talent for getting opera singers to act, especially to indulge in a great deal of uninstructed physical contact, tender, passionate or brutal, audiences, including critics, were bowled over by many incidental touches, which served to distract them from the incoherence of the overall 'concept' of the production. And it goes without saying that after an initial shock-horror response to Boulez's anti-emotional conducting, they were flattered at being introduced to a Wagner whose existence they hadn't previously suspected, one whose social message is conveyed by lengthy stretches of detached presentation punctuated by rare moments of uninhibited physical action.

I dwell on the production, which moved from provoking physical violence in 1976 to unqualified triumph in 1981, to indicate what has been a major shift in approaches to Wagner during the last couple of decades. Unavoidable as a pervasive musical presence, deeply embarrassing as drama, Wagner was, so to speak, waiting to be *aufgehoben*. And as soon as Boulez and Chéreau had effected the trick, the 'serious' public breathed a long-pent-up sigh of relief. He could be heard as a supreme musical innovator, while his dramas could easily be freed from the constraints of universality with which Wagner had megalo-maniacally encumbered them, and contemplated as character-istic social statements, on a par with middle-period Ibsen (a connection which Thomas Mann had already made in his famous address of 1933). Bayreuth was at last free from the stigma of being the 'Home of Tradition', once its proudest boast, and became a 'workshop' (they were just coming in then), the leading instantiation of that fashionable concept of the last quarter-century. It means roughly that anything goes as long as it can be seen to be in a state of evolution, i.e. lack of preparation, and vaguely in line with bourgeois notions of what Marxism comes to – at least on the stage. To express regret at the passing of a period in which Wagner's dramas were seen as expressions of what their creator had called the 'purely human' was to align oneself with complacent stagnation – and wasn't Wagner him-self the arch-revolutionary of his time?

Furthermore, these innovations in Wagner performance coincided with the dissemination of attacks on 'essentialist humanism' and vaguely synonymous terms, and so with the adoption of the notion that every aspect of human nature is socially constructed, and thus inalienably linked to the circum-stances of its production. After 1968 'timeless truths' went sharply out of fashion, and performers, producers, conductors who were intent on showing their timeliness seized the oppor-tunity. Chéreau's influence in this department has been greater than Boulez's. Whereas many conductors perform the *Ring* as if they had never heard Boulez do it, all directors either follow in the wake of Chéreau, taking things to ever greater extremes, or else brace themselves for retailing what they know will be categorised on sight as 'traditional', though it has been in abeyance long enough now for its replacements to have usurped the term, even if, naturally, they don't want to; since they always see themselves as radical, subversive and so forth.

Is it fair to Chéreau and the breed of directors of whom he is a member, and in Wagnerian production a progenitor, to say that they domesticate Wagner? In one sense it clearly is not. For the aim was to shock: instead of attending performances of Wagner's works which were to all intents and purposes indistinguishable, and which thus ministered to their being regarded as ritual occasions, the audiences were to be forced to think, at least to the extent of making articulate to themselves the different impression what they were seeing (and probably hearing) made on them from what they were used to. On the other hand, the rate at which audiences get accustomed to style of direction, that is stop reflecting on the novel import of what they are seeing, may have dismayed the directors at least as much as it gratified them. The absorption of new production styles at Bayreuth provides a strange footnote to the burgeoning subject of Wagner reception. Directors have found themselves forced to move away from the nineteenth century, even though the idea that a work should be staged as occurring in the time when it was written continues, for all its inanity, to be a shibboleth of contemporary theatre. So Wagner's works are increasingly being set in the present, or the future, one or another future, relocated on various planets, or back to nowhere in particular. At which point the only main difference between their conception and Wieland Wagner's – he who wanted to realise his grandfather's ideal of the purely human by freeing the settings from a 'mythological' aura which irresistibly suggested a particular period's idea of what mythological space and time looked like – is that he was still passionately concerned to create beautiful visual impressions, and they are passionately concerned not to. In the interests of communicating the horrors of an industrialised, late-capitalist world it is necessary to make the sets repellent and gaudy, or simply depressing; and the manifest use of advanced technology which draws attention to itself serves also to conjure up vague thoughts of self-referentiality, if the audience has heard of that.

It is difficult to write about recent developments in Wagner production without sounding polemical, even if one wanted not to. It is necessary to say, it seems, that insofar as the directors and their complicit conductors and obedient singing actors, or more likely acting singers, think that they are getting their audiences to ponder on political issues, they are mistaken. The most that they can do is to give the audience, which inevitably remains largely middle class or above, the gratifying sense that they are witnessing a 'relevant' production of Wagner, while they enjoy the music in the old way, so far as that is possible while they keep their eyes open. Who has been led to reflect more seriously or deeply on the evils of industrialism through seeing a post-Chéreau *Ring*, as opposed to a 'traditional' one in which Nibelheim was depicted realistically, and contrasted starkly with the rocky heights on which the scenes either side of Wotan and Loge's visit to Nibelheim take place? Who, even, among the professional critics who have written about such productions of the *Ring*, has come out with any striking new ideas about it? They tend merely to report on the latest would-be scandalous 'concepts' purveyed by directors dressing up their clapped-out ideology in thinly new guises, and to leave it at that. One kind of mindlessness is replaced by another, and the transition is taken for thought.

It is for this reason that I claim that Wagner has been domesticated. Every attempt to make him relevant by portraying his characters as more like our politicians, or ourselves, merely reduces the stature of his work without enhancing ours. The latest *Ring* production which I saw in Bayreuth, already available on CD, video and laser-disc as I write, was directed by Harry Kupfer, and as is now routine it depicted the gods as, from the start, a set of trilby-hatted gangsters, carrying transparent, empty, and when they caught the light, dazzling (symbolism!) suitcases, and entering a kitschy neon-lit Valhalla in a state of drunkenness, and so forth; and it ended with Brünnhilde getting a nuclear holocaust under way (by igniting Siegfried's funeral pyre), while the bourgeoisie dragged on their TV sets and watched the end of civilisation as they sipped their glasses of Sekt. Such a commentary on the media-potential of all catastrophes (though the nuclear holocaust would probably defy attempts to televise it) is a point worth making, or remaking. But not, I think, a point to be made at the end of the *Ring*, where it not only jars with Wagner's orchestral peroration, but altogether deflects attention from it. The grandeur of those closing minutes is something to be pondered at length, but it has to be experienced in the first place, not sabotaged. To eliminate the experience is to give us nothing to ponder on – though I admit that the relationship between artistic experience and reflection on it is a complex matter. But whatever the final truth may be about the relationship between feeling and the 'synthesising intellect', there must first be feeling. Everyone who has had powerful artistic experiences knows how difficult it is to remain true to them when trying to give an account of what they really came to – it is the first and last test of the true critic. But what many contemporary directors do is to barge in and insert the criticism into the work itself, insulting both the creator and his audience. Wagner, as we shall see, eliminated an important section of Brünnhilde's final address in *Götterdämmerung* because he came to regard it as 'too didactic'. It is not for us to supply what he eliminated.

5

Grandeur and Suffering in Wagner:
Some Case Studies

The claims that are made by Wagner's domesticators, which I enumerated in the last chapter, are not to be lightly dismissed, if only because so many intelligent people believe them. But I don't intend to confront them directly, and in general terms. Rather I shall look at some particular cases of Wagner's presentation of what he undoubtedly saw as the human condition, and leave readers, who would be engaged in a pointless exercise if they were not also listeners, to draw their own conclusions.

There is no question that Wagner uses all his resources to depict figures who are larger than life. That is something that is also true of Homer, Shakespeare, and many other great epic and dramatic artists. Why do they do it? Does it serve a useful, as opposed to a thrilling or wish-fulfilling purpose? A simple question to which there is no simple answer. It seems to be felt that in the case of Homer and the Greek tragedians, if not of Shakespeare and Racine, there is no real issue to be confronted, because they lived in a period when it was in some way more natural to see life in those terms, as containing heroes whose dimensions were justified, permissible. They were thought, or thought themselves, to be living under a group of gods who gave them a status which can't be claimed for men who live in a secular world, or under a Christian dispensation, where there may be saints, but not heroes. Some of Wagner's characters think that they are living in the same kind of world as the Greek heroes, with gods in charge of their destinies, but Wagner didn't believe in those gods, as Homer presumably did. Does that fact in itself make the crucial difference? It seems that it does, because the whole portrayal of the relationship between gods and men in Wagner betrays his self-consciousness about the nature of mythology.

He is often, I think rightly, praised for the prodigious labours of research that he undertook into Norse and Germanic myths before he distilled their essence for his purposes. But that can also be taken in a different way, as showing a mistaken attitude towards myth in general. For Wagner was a very sophisticated, very intellectual person, and his raids on ancient myths resulted in a product that was so far from the spirit of the original that it is not difficult to argue that it merely cosmeticises, with enormous skill and still greater panache, stories containing contemporaneous figures or rather types, whose predicaments are not seriously to be illuminated by placing them in some contrived mythical dimension.

That, yet again, is the gravamen of Nietzsche's charge against Wagner, when he caustically remarks, ' "But the *content* of the Wagnerian texts! their mythic content! their eternal content!" – Question: how can we test this content, this eternal content? – The chemist replies: translate Wagner into reality, into the modern – let us be even crueller – into the bourgeois! What becomes of Wagner then? – Among ourselves, I have tried it . . . Would you believe it? all of Wagner's heroines, without exception, as soon as they are stripped of their heroic skin, become almost indistinguishable from Madame Bovary! . . . Indeed, transposed into hugeness, Wagner does not seem to be interested in any problems except those which now occupy the little decadents of Paris. Always five steps from the hospital. All of them entirely modern, entirely *metropolitan* problems. Don't doubt it.' (*The Case of Wagner*, section 9). And he enumerates Wagner's central figures, making parallels with ones in contemporary life and literature.

It is a game that Nietzsche is expert at playing, one of his fundamental strategies for dealing with the depressing nature of the world he saw surrounding him. Yet it is not a hard game to play; its chief snag, after a time, seems to be that it is too hard to lose. Why is Nietzsche prepared to trivialise and reduce Siegfried and Parsifal, but not Achilles, as Homer presents him in the *Iliad*? For this great hero, the centre of the world's most powerful epic, is engaged for most of its course in a sulk, induced by Agamemnon's unsporting refusal to let him have the spoils of war that he has earned. Must heroes always be heroic? Evidently not, if Achilles is one of them, and if not he, who?

The concept of the heroic clearly has to do with the way in which people are seen, not just with them in themselves. To the mean in spirit, nothing is heroic or worthwhile. Nietzsche was not *au fond* a mean-spirited man, but for his polemical purposes he was prepared, on occasion, to behave as if he were. He wanted to show his age (which is ours, only we might have rendered him speechless) that it was small, and so when it appeared to be large, as with Wagner's creations, he had to show that there was something counterfeit about them. Even though the techniques are crude, they force us into thinking about what the criteria for greatness of soul are, and under what conditions they can be fulfilled.

Nietzsche's strictures on Wagner are often accepted because we are embarrassed, now, at the mere thought of the heroic. We can, like him, accept it if the works in which it is incarnated are sufficiently remote, so that we become anthropologists in time, happy to grant a status to distant figures which we would never accord to ones nearer to us. Shake-speare, who was once thought to have invested a good deal in the heroic, is now felt to have hedged his heroes – Hamlet, Othello, Coriolanus, Antony – about with so many qualifica-tions that we can cope with them as fascinating studies in immaturity, self-glorification, self-ignorance, and other things that make us feel comfortable. Wagner, by sharp and damag-ing contrast, has no reservations about his – not that he thinks them perfect, which everyone would agree would make them uninteresting, but about the scale of whatever qualities they possess. And yet his art seems to fit into the period in which it was created with a snugness which leads us to wonder how he can have lived in the centre of the age of the novel, that supreme form of the unheroic, and not shown more suspicion of his characters and the ambience he created for them to live in.

Let's look cursorily at the central figures in his dramas, see which seem to have accorded to them heroic status, and then focus on some particular case. *Der fliegende Holländer*: the Dutchman himself, and Senta. *Tannhäuser*: the only candidate is the eponymous central figure, and as we shall see, he is marginal in one way to Wagner's work, though central by intention. *Lohengrin*: again only the central figure, who may not be all that central. *Tristan und Isolde*: the two central figures. *Die Meistersinger*: no one, or perhaps Hans Sachs if we widen our criteria. The *Ring*: Siegmund, Brünnhilde, Sieg-fried, and perhaps Alberich. Wotan, as a god, and the dominat-ing figure in the *Ring*, can be included if the contrast of gods and heroes is not taken as sacrosanct. *Parsifal*: the central figure.

So first back to the Dutchman, and the woman who saves him. How impressive a figure is Wagner's first serious attempt to portray a man of heroic proportions? In the first place, as

I remarked earlier, Wagner's interest is typically in someone who has done something frightful but not straightforwardly evil – which is to say that he himself suffers more than anyone else on account of his action. The Dutchman's oath to round the Cape at all costs is a blasphemy for which Satan punishes him. It is, again characteristically, an assertion of will taken with no regard to consequences – here Wagner's heroes tally with ancient ones in their rashness, pursuing a goal without reckoning the cost. We now, living in what Adorno called with horror 'the administered society', are bound to regard things from the standpoint of accountants, wearily but tirelessly carrying out cost-benefit analyses. But we do look with nostalgia at people who were not so placed, and try to find areas of life where we might behave in this way ourselves. Hence the attraction of (literally) daredevil figures, and also no doubt the cult of the gangster-hero. And our imaginations also are caught by figures who are prepared to risk anything to get home – hence the permanent attractiveness of Odysseus. The Dutchman is one such, but the horror of his situation is that in his determination he vowed the very thing which would ensure that he never did get home – at least, not until he died, a consummation that Satan denies him.

That is the figure whom we encounter when he makes his first appearance, coming onto land again after seven years. He is set up to appear in the most glamorous light, since all we have had after the Overture and some 'Halloho'-ing from Daland's crew is the mundane conversation between Daland, one of Wagner's most pithy portrayals of venality, and the charming Steersman, who falls asleep on watch while singing a catchy song to his girlfriend. As the Dutchman emerges, Wagner changes the atmosphere completely, with quiet, slumping strings alternating with lugubrious low winds. At last the Dutchman mutters his opening line, 'Die Frist ist um'

(The time is up), and we are launched on the first of Wagner's succession of monologues of exhaustion, a line which will continue through Tannhäuser's Rome Narration in Act III; Tristan's mighty pair of self-analyses in Act III; Siegmund's in Act I, and Wotan's vast act of self-communing in Act II of *Die Walküre*; Amfortas's in Acts I and III of *Parsifal*, as well as Parsifal's own in Act III. All of these monologues fall into sections in which understanding the plight the respective characters got into alternates with hopes and ideas for its alleviation, and further descents into despair at the impossibility of emergence. What is remarkable is the maturity of expression which the Dutchman's plight forces Wagner to employ.

In the first section he rails, in recitative punctuated by rushing strings, at the 'proud ocean's' throwing him up on land, only to lay claim to him once more after a brief spell; and he sings in more eloquent declamation of his eternal torment, lasting 'bis ... euer letztes Nass versiegt!' (until you are drained dry!). The strings begin their restless heaving, as in the overture, which connotes the Dutchman's travels, and he recalls how often he has sought death, driving his ship onto rocks, but always to no avail. To a despairing octave descent he cries, as so many of his successors will, 'Nirgends ein Grab!' (Nowhere a grave!), the dread command of damnation.

Four bars of pianissimo timpani rolls follow, always a portent of climactic anguish in Wagner, as at last the Dutchman begins a long, upward-moving melody of hopeless yearning: 'Dich frage ich, gepries' ner Engel Gottes' (I ask you, blessed angel of God), a huge span which contradicts the despair from which it arises, but is cut off, in further cries of the futility of finding anyone on earth who will be faithful. After an orchestral outburst, still more strident, another theme of hope emerges, but now with impressive momentum; this time the hope is that the Day of Judgement will eventually arrive, when all things, even torment, will come to an end. And with a final effort the Dutchman sings 'Ew'ge Vernichtung nimm mich auf!' (Eternal destruction take me away!), a sentiment his crew echoes in a ghostly whisper.

This scena, which lasts more than a quarter of an hour, breaks new ground both in its dimensions – all the more striking in a relatively concise work, Wagner's shortest by some way – and in its unremitting intensity. Great laments had been the order of the day since the birth of opera, but not on this scale, and not on this subject. The Dutchman's plight is unconnected with any other person, though it is only another, as yet unspecified, person who will rescue him. He is, in the most basic terms, doomed to live, so unwillingly charged with energy that the peace he longs for is unimaginable. Apart from the qualifications for mythic, heroic stature which I have already noted, he has the all-important further one of not being presented with psychological depth – indeed psychology doesn't come into it. That is no doubt the main reason for Wagner's failing to give him a name; in the legend he is usually known as Vanderdecken, but here he simply *is* his defining characteristic. What we sympathise with – and I am taking it that we do feel sympathy – is a predicament, rather than a person. It is noteworthy that contemporary producers have gone in for various 'interpretations' of the opera, according to which it is someone or other's dream, favoured candidates being Senta and the Steersman. But the Dutchman himself has been left alone: he is simply presented as a given, and there is nothing that producers can do about that. Although making the opera into a dream of the Steersman seems merely to trivialise it, making it into a dream of Senta's seems more promising, because she is quite easily seen as a psychological study. Set in her social context, as the Dutchman very evidently isn't (he doesn't have one), we are led, if we have that kind of interest, into wondering why she alone, among the spinning maidens, is obsessed by the portrait of the Dutchman, why she finds her suitor Erik so boring, why she wants to devote herself to so foolhardy an endeavour as saving a man who may only be the subject of a ballad.

At the same time, the tendency recent producers have shown to rewrite Wagner's drama for him reveals that they can't believe that, as it stands, it can command the interest of contemporary audiences. Although the Dutchman is manifestly the central figure, they want him to be a wish-fulfilment, a projection, because he has no individuating psychological features. But to adopt their procedure is to beg the question: Is it possible now, or was it possible in 1842, to make a serious contribution to our understanding of anything by creating or re-animating a myth? I can't see that the answer is so obviously negative that such creative adaptations of Wagner have to be made. The Satan-defying vow that the Dutchman has taken in the indefinitely distant past can be understood, was surely meant to be understood, as an act of typicality: something which one might have done, and which would determine that one would never find peace. To see life in such terms is not any longer something which most of us can manage; yet with his incomparable imaginative vitality and musical resources Wagner has rendered the possibility open to us. What Wagner is offering us, and what we are apparently unable to accept, is a vision of life in which we perform an act which can't be gone back on and which sets the pattern for the whole of the rest of our existence. And if that existence is ghastly, the only hope is that we might find another person who is unconditionally ready to offer themself in order to free us.

But supposing there were such a person, how would the

mechanism of salvation be effected? Beethoven, who was pre-occupied with the same issue in his only drama, made it a straightforward matter of rescuing someone from imprisonment, no joke given the circumstances, but thoroughly intelligible in terms of what Leonore has to do. But Wagner is concerned with a different question, one which he devoted his life to locating and then trying to solve. He had, one can deduce from all the dramas, quite apart from the copious evidence of what he wrote in his discursive essays, the strongest sense that life as it is ordinarily lived, and apart from any specific set of social or political conditions, is not worth the pains and efforts that are involved. But to transcend the normal terms of life is inevitably to offend against community, and even in some way to offend against the constitution of the self, which depends on the community whose codes it needs to violate. His characters are often accused of being morbidly, or wickedly, self-obsessed. But the Dutchman, who could hardly be obsessed with anyone else, gives us in a virtually diagrammatic form a grasp of how inevitable that self-obsession is. By chance or instinct, Wagner hit upon as his first hero a person who represented for him the fundamental human lot, which is one of terrifying isolation.

The most obvious way, at least for the last few centuries, in which one might hope to overcome that isolation, if there is no religious option open to one – or even, maybe, if there is – is by erotic passion. That is not what the Dutchman wants, because it presupposes that life is worth living – it makes life worth living, or that is the idea. But the Dutchman can only see life, as his creator often only could, in terms of fearful striving. So his search, a highly original one in Western culture, is for someone who will enable him to die by dying herself, to show that she cares about him in the way he most wants to be cared about.

But at least as strong in Wagner's make-up was the attraction of Romantic love, the idea that life could be made worth living if it achieved a pitch of incessant ecstasy. That is what his next central figure hopes to achieve. *Tannhäuser* is, all told, Wagner's least successful work, but like the failures of other great artists, it is deeply illuminating to consider why. It is also interesting, and revealing, that Wagner never put his finger on the reasons for its unsatisfactoriness, thinking until the end that it was a matter of failure in getting the details right, rather than, as is in fact the case, a fundamentally flawed conception – his only one. The flaw is clearly seen in the broken-backed character of Tannhäuser himself, a passive figure of a kind that Wagner was not able to understand. True, Tannhäuser has, before the opera opens, taken a pretty big initiative: he has left the court of minstrels to which he belongs, finding it, as he is right to do, desperately insipid. Furthermore, he has gone to the Venusberg, the very seat of sin, and has made the most of the opportunities it offers, for an unspecified period.

The Overture, one of the Victorians' favourite pieces, sets out the terms of the drama, or rather what Wagner took them to be, with unusual clarity. It begins with the Pilgrims' Chorus, solemnly intoned by woodwinds; after the first time through, the 'cellos enter with a heart-weary figure which immediately suggests the individual's burden of sorrow. Typically, it rises only in order to fall, as though the weight were indeed too much for it. The pilgrims' music re-enters in brassy glory, this time with the excited accompanying motif which Wagner called 'the pulse of life' on the strings, and then peters out in mid-phrase, and the wicked part begins. Wagner's first grown-up depiction of sensuality is highly effective: darting, tumescent, chromatic figures, flickering accompaniments, suggestive of flames consuming the soul. And in its original form the Overture ends with a further thundering out of the pilgrims' hymn.

If it sounds a bit corny now, compared to the eternal freshness of the *Holländer* Overture, it is still easy to 'read' and to feel that it serves its purpose. Although Wagner gives the pilgrims an easy victory in it, he skilfully conveys an ambivalence in the Venus central section. It has colouristic allure, and yet isn't something one could live with for long. And the ballet which succeeds it in the original (1845) version is a short-winded affair, more of the same and failing to add anything. Wagner is not, despite his reputation, particularly good at depicting mere sensuality. Here, at any rate, his portrayal of post-coital *tristesse* is more convincing, indeed the slow encroachment of languour over the whole scene is striking enough to make Tannhäuser's confession of weariness to Venus superfluous. Nor is her attempt to rekindle his interest in the least satisfactory. The composer himself correctly came to feel that it was the weakest music he had composed. Tannhäuser tries to rise to the occasion in his celebrated Hymn to Venus, already heard twice in the Overture, but once more there is a lack of conviction in it, no doubt partly intentional; also, I can't help thinking, partly not. Wagner has trapped himself, as it were, between idioms. The music of the pilgrims, conventional in its piety, is one pole of *Tannhäuser*; that of the Venusberg, disturbingly chromatic, the other. Tannhäuser, caught in his allegiance between the two, has no idiom of his own, and his praise of Venus is as foursquare as it is hectic, employing one kind of means to celebrate another kind of end. Because Wagner has contrasted the two worlds between which he is torn so comprehensively, he is left without a convincing musical idiom for characterising his would-be hero, who is attracted to both. So, at least until his great Narration in Act III, Tannhäuser remains the one figure in Wagner on whom we can get no purchase.

Wagner wanted to contrast, it is all too plain, two kinds of love: sensual and spiritual. In doing, or trying to do, that, he showed himself to be an obedient child of his age in a way which is surprising and disconcerting. He often said, in later life, that the basic form of love was that between the sexes – an anti-Schopenhauerian claim which he disarmingly presented as a 'modification' of Schopenhauer. The great pessimist actually saw sexual love as the most blatant form of the Will to Live, which is in his view the root of all evil. Although Wagner had not yet read or heard of Schopenhauer when he wrote *Tannhäuser*, it tries to be a Schopenhauerian work. It fails, not as one might expect, by inadvertently glorifying the flesh, and making the spirit seem insipid. It is somewhat more complicated than that, since the heroine Elisabeth is no mere representative of spiritual, i.e. Christian, love. She is, in fact, against all expectation the major success of the work. But she is that interesting kind of success that ruins the work in which it occurs. She is the adored of all at the court in the Wartburg, but there is more to her than meets any of their eyes. They are so high-minded a crew that it is surprising they manage to reproduce themselves, as Tannhäuser acidly observes. Sanctimonious, self-righteous, vying with one another in the Contest of Song to celebrate chastity, it is not in the least puzzling that Tannhäuser finds them insufferable, and is driven by their songs to launch into his paean of praise, this time coming from the heart, to Venus. And Wagner shows them in the most vindictive light in their reaction to him. They round on him, swords drawn, and only Elisabeth's superb moment of interjection saves Tannhäuser's life.

That Elisabeth incarnates a conception of love that doesn't regard the body as something to be frightened of is made clear

even before she actually appears for her famous Entrance Aria
in Act II. The orchestral introduction to it, which is often
fidgeted through while audiences wait for the prima donna to
arrive, is not only fine music but shows a lot about her character. After its opening, which takes up the concluding joyful
strains of Act I, when the minstrels welcomed Tannhäuser's
return from they know not where, there is a feverish passage
for the violins and violas which should advert us to the fact
that Elisabeth's excitement is no mere maidenly relief at the
prospect of seeing an old friend again. In fact it is quite as
erotically charged as any of the goings-on in the Venusberg,
at any rate in the 1845 version. And when Elisabeth finally
does launch her aria, it may be primarily directed to the Hall
of Song, but her enthusiasm for that location would be excessive if she weren't filled with the prospect of seeing *him* in it,
and the music leaps obligingly when she sings of her increasing
heart-rate.

The drop in musical and dramatic temperature when
Tannhäuser arrives is in the first place indicative of the embarrassment both he and Elisabeth feel on being reunited, and
given that he has to guard his secret, it is only to be expected
that he should remain rather stiff, though one suspects once
more that Wagner is at a loss for means to characterise a man
without qualities. Anyway the main burden of the duet falls
to Elisabeth, who tells Tannhäuser that while she used to
listen to the other minstrels with pleasure, when she heard
him singing, 'Bald wollt' es mich wie Schmerz durchbeben,
bald drang's in mich wie jähe Lust. Gefühle, die ich nie
empfunden! Verlangen, das ich nie gekannt!' (Now it would
thrill through me like pain, now penetrate me with sudden
joy. Feelings I had never experienced! Longings that were
strange to me!) She goes on to say that she had been anxious
about the effect of his songs, but he tells her to praise 'den

75

Gott der Liebe' (the God of Love), using the masculine form
rather disingenuously, since he is certainly not talking about
the Christian God.

The Contest of Song follows, after the popular ceremonials
which Wagner could produce with such warmth of appeal.
But after Wolfram has delivered his elevated sentiments
Tannhäuser comes into his own, linguistically and argumenta-
tively if not musically. He points out, in apparent ignorance
of the traditions of lofty hyperbole practised in these circles,
that the terms in which Wolfram has characterised love should
be reserved for God, that to talk of worship is to talk of the
untouchable. Warming to his theme, Tannhäuser goes on to
say that his interest is in the palpable, 'was sich aus gleichem
Stoff erzeuget, in weicher Formung an euch schmiegt, ich
nah' ihm kühn, der Quell der Wonnen' (what is constituted
of the selfsame stuff, in weaker mould nestles to one – I boldly
approach the fount of delight), and more to even stronger
effect. This is excellent discussion, but abstract and not something that Wagner could set to music which would seem
appropriate. The first half of Tannhäuser's reply is semi-bald
recitative, the second half flowing but irrelevant lyricism. It
upsets the company, however, who have followed it more
closely than one imagines audiences in the theatre ever doing,
and Tannhäuser is accused of blasphemy by the beastly
Biterolf, succinctly hit off in his mean-spirited primness by
Wagner. Accusations and counter-accusations begin to fly
around, though still at a level which leaves the musician in
Wagner floundering. It is only when Tannhäuser throws cau-
tion to the winds that Wagner is able to marshal his resources,
albeit traditional ones, to produce a reaction of revulsion from
the court which rings true.

The full-scale unmasking of the minstrels and their attendants as a collection of smug ignoramuses must have given

Wagner great satisfaction, but having failed to present a plausible Venus in Act I, and created this insufferable and claustrophobic society in Act II, it is unclear what Tannhäuser is torn between. Insofar as Wagner manages to create him at all, it is as an *homme moyen sensuel*, but Wagner is never interested in them, so he felt, as someone who was only drawn to extremes, that his hero must have nothing of the *moyen* about him. Whereas his true heroes tend to the demonic, or the radiantly spontaneous, Tannhäuser has about him a passivity of character, even if, as with many fundamentally passive people, he is given to violent outbursts to prove that he is a genuine agent. When Elisabeth steps between him and his would-be murderers, we are much more moved by the tensions within her, genuine and nearly uncontrollable, than by her relation to this broken reed who is only worthy of her protection because the crowd of assailants is so detestable.

The passage in which she defends him, rounding on these cruel would-be judges, is great drama, wonderfully set, and in isolation perhaps the finest thing Wagner had yet achieved. And when she sings, 'Seht mich, die Jungfrau, deren Blüte mit einem jähen Schlag er brach, die ihn geliebt tief im Gemüte, der jubelnd er das Herz zerstach!' (See me, the maid whom he broke in one quick blow in her youth, who bore him deep love in her soul, whose heart he exalted in piercing!), there is no question that Wagner has found a character whose inmost being he can create in superb words and shattering music. No wonder the company is humbled, singing in praise of her with utter conviction, though they have inevitably to turn her into 'an angel' to do it. But this is the grandest of all grand opera ensembles, huge and justified in its massiveness. With all its longueurs and ineffectualities, *Tannhäuser* is an indispensable work for the completeness with which Wagner has created, against heavy odds, a heroine in whose realisation there is no false note.

The reason why Wagner is so successful with Elisabeth, much more even than with the heroines who immediately succeed and follow her, Senta and Elsa, is that she is both vulnerable and courageous, and that those qualities spring from a single and deep source: her desire for Tannhäuser, which she can acknowledge even though it goes against the ethos of her society. We have seen that she was troubled by it, in her scene with Tannhäuser; but what upset her was that she didn't understand her feelings, not that she thought them wicked. By the time we get to Act III, Wagner seems to have realised that the dramatic balance of the work has been lost. Tannhäuser has to be made interesting, and for that to occur it seems that Elisabeth has to be made uninteresting. At any rate what happens is that after a long and very graphic Prelude, of a kind unique in Wagner – it amounts to a travelogue, the precise content of which we learn only later – which forcefully redirects our attention to Tannhäuser, there is a scene between Wolfram and Elisabeth in which they try to outdo one another in selfless concern, and before she makes her departure Elisabeth has her second aria, this time a prayer to the Virgin, in which she seems to have forgotten what her personality is, and to have become a full member of the Wartburg society. 'Make me, pure and angel-like, enter into thy blessed realm,' she begs, and hopes that she has managed to 'kill' all sinful longings. This is no longer the Elisabeth whom we admired in Act II for having the courage of her strong feelings, but a new creation, designed to make us remember that the subject of the opera is the battle for Tannhäuser's soul. The music Wagner awards her here is of a predictable kind, virginity being best expressed by oboes and other pure-sounding wind instruments. It is not a boring number, quite, but it is impossible not to feel that Wagner has disowned his most convincing female creation to date. The atmosphere of sanctimony, though it is not of the spiteful variety we witnessed in Act II, is carried still further by Wolfram's launching into his apostrophe to the Evening Star (Venus, of course, but the point is not laboured, or perhaps even made). Such conventionalities would be hard to forgive if they were not the preparation for something truly momentous; Wagner's musical dramaturgy is hardly subtle here, but it packs a punch. As the suave melody of Wolfram's prayer comes to its end, it is cut off by a jagged, assertive but desperate phrase which marks the return, once more, of Tannhäuser, but from the opposite direction to Act I – from Rome, where he has gone, under orders, to seek absolution, only to receive as unforgiving a reception from the Pope as he had from the denizens of the Wartburg. No wonder he feels that he might just as well have stayed at home. But his religious damnation, as at this stage it seems to be, is his dramatic salvation. As an unabsolved penitent he has at last acquired a personality, even if it is still at bottom a reactive one. Bored in the company of Venus, he was boring. Contemptuous of the prigs in the Wartburg, he was abstract, then ranting. But rejected by the Pope, he has gained his own idiom of bitterness and recrimination. His long Narration, though it comes too late to retrospectively revivify him, or make him heroic, at least makes him interesting, as justifiably embittered people are. His wilful decision to return to Venus, who is more likely to be forgiving than any of the Christians he has encountered, is expressed in a cry that comes from depths he has only recently discovered, or been forced to create. The struggle that ensues between Wolfram and Venus, the latter making a surprise guest appearance, is compelling drama, though once more we feel that the person who shouts loudest for him will win, and his final abdication of agency makes him little more than a sad carcase to be fought over. The dénouement is swiftly effected by Elisabeth's having died in the meanwhile and having her prayers answered by God, once more prepared to accept a sacrificial victim. Wagner grafts onto a most un-*Holländer*-like action the same conclusion, except that things are much more explicitly Christian here.

Commentators who feel that Tannhäuser's plight is not as fascinating as it might be have tended to see in the work Wagner's dramatising of the artist at loggerheads with his society, but that was a theme he was not to take up till later. Wagner himself said that Tannhäuser was a human being, Wolfram being a poet. But if he intended to create in Tannhäuser a purely human figure, in his sense, one can only say that on this occasion he portrayed the average rather than the mythically typical. No doubt myths have their simplicities, but *Tannhäuser* is crudely schematic, as the character of Elisabeth, at least in Act II, reveals by contrast. If Wagner was really concerned with the duality of flesh and spirit – it seems to me to be one of his distinctions that he was not, or was much less concerned than the vast majority of victims of the Platonic-Christian tradition – then he stumbled on the solution in his creation of Elisabeth, only to fail to recognise that he had, or to go back on it because it robbed him of his subject-matter. But in fact the central unsatisfactoriness of *Tannhäuser* shows that he was not dealing with an issue which mattered to him: hence the cardboard nature of Venus and the minstrels, and therefore of the man who is undecided between them.

Some of this became plain to him when he came to rethink and rewrite the opera for Paris at the beginning of the eighteen-sixties. He felt that Venus and her environment needed more sophisticated and extended treatment, which was true.

But while the music and the added text which he created then are hideously impressive – there is no more disturbing music than the revised version of the Venusberg scene, which colonises, with repulsive success, the realm of pathological sexuality – he failed to make appropriate adjustments elsewhere. Admittedly he was, in the first place, providing a ballet to gratify his Parisian audience, but his artistic integrity would never have allowed him to do merely that. But the crucial cause of unease – the status of Tannhäuser – was left untouched. Anyone who could survive, as he does, the orgies of the revised Venusberg clearly has remarkable stamina, and his decision to move to a healthier climate becomes more plausible. But what balance the work had before – one kind of inadequacy countering another – was ruined. There is no need to make a fuss about stylistic incongruities, since it is entirely in keeping with the Venusberg that its idiom should be so decadently sophisticated, and what immediately follows it, the song of the Shepherd, is the more moving by virtue of its fresh innocence. But the Wartburg music is rendered still more colourless, so that Tannhäuser is now caught between the devil and the shallow grey sea. Meanwhile, the character of Elisabeth remains unaffected by the changes that were made elsewhere. She emerges, somewhat to one's surprise, as the most completely drawn woman in Wagner until Sieglinde in *Die Walküre*, and in a few economical but confident strokes. She rarely receives her due, perhaps because her creator betrayed her in Act III. But listen to the first and last twenty minutes of Act II, and there is a figure of rare delicacy and strength.

What Wagner was probably trying to create in Tannhäuser was one of his ongoing succession of characters plagued by almost unendurable guilt, but the evidence (in the work) is that abandonment to sexual excess is not a fault which he could really believe to be all that bad, especially in view of the unappetising alternative. So whereas in his first drama the interest resides in the doomed man, and only secondarily in his redemptrix, the situation is reversed in *Tannhäuser*.

6

Lohengrin and its Prelude

In Wagner's next work, the last of what could be called his trilogy, where he is looking for themes to match the musical resources and inspiration which he could only realise in drama – but what drama? – it becomes unclear who is redeeming whom, and from what. Wagner's whole art, as I have suggested, springs from a radical dissatisfaction with life, but the sources of that dissatisfaction lay so deep that he had the greatest difficulty in finding an adequate situation to embody it. The first shot was closer to the mark than the second; for Wagner is not primarily interested in people who can't decide between two alternatives, but rather in ones for whom life is comprehensively wretched because they can't find in the world anything which answers to their sense of how life can possibly be worth living. Making an irreversible decision seems to be as 'existential' a deed as one can perform, but for the Dutchman it only perpetuates a state which he was trying to escape from. Wagner's characters are as fascinated by and attracted to immortality as most people are, but most inquisitive as to what it might consist in. They are insistent on having life on their own terms, but they haven't got the understanding of themselves which would enable them to express what those terms are. They have to live first, find out what their mistakes were, and then see if they can live again. In other words, they are like any deeply reflective person, which is a large part of the appeal which they continue to exercise over our imaginations.

Where they are unlike the majority of people is that they take up a 'do or die' attitude, locating the value which will alone justify their lives in a circumscribed mode of being which is extrapolated to infinity. Their attitude towards death thus becomes complex in a unique kind of way. What they would be truly satisfied by is a mode of existence which would still seem worthwhile if it lasted for ever. One of the reasons that so many of Wagner's major characters want to die is that they are worthy of something more fulfilling than simply life. But to see death as that – and there doesn't seem to be a third option – they also need to embrace some pretty heady form of metaphysics, according to which this life is only a phase in one's existence. Wagner's *oeuvre* consists of a survey of the possibilities.

But in his third opera, *Lohengrin*, he is evidently stalling. Or, to put it more charitably, Wagner is composing a work which will give him the possibility of discovering what might satisfy him, as an artist. The Prelude to Act I, that miraculous piece in which Wagner first reveals the full extent of his magical powers in handling the orchestra, hardly suggests the terms of the drama which is to follow – it is, in fact, in its mono-thematicism, a negation of the possibility of drama. Beginning with exquisite string and wind chords, breathing themselves into existence, by the time it has come to its serene conclusion, after spinning itself out, its theme descending through the full orchestra until it reaches its consummating climax (but it has no hint of the erotic about it), we feel that we have heard a self-sufficient piece, modest in dimensions but of limitless beauty. What kind of drama can it be setting the scene for? All Wagner's other preludes and overtures propel us into the works whose tone they set, even if they don't set up the terms of a conflict, which is what they almost always do. Even the Prelude to *Tristan und Isolde*, which if not monothematic is nonetheless a piece in which each theme bears the most intimate relation to the others, is something which one couldn't, or shouldn't, be able to bear by itself. It establishes so potent a mood of longing that we know, even the first time round, that we are in for a drama of extreme suspense – the Prelude, for all the power of its climax, which so many subsequent composers have hopelessly taken as a model, leaves us with the feeling that we must go on until the frustration implicit in that climax has been dispelled. All the other preludes and overtures either consist of many of the major themes of the subsequent musical drama, as in *Der fliegende Holländer*, *Tannhäuser*, *Die Meistersinger* and *Parsifal*, or establish the mood of the act which is to follow, as in the preludes to each part of the *Ring*.

The Prelude to *Lohengrin* is not, then, promising, because it makes no promises that it doesn't promptly fulfil. And when the curtain rises and the action begins we have, for some time, good reason for apprehensiveness. Wagner, no doubt with calculation, brings us down with a rude bump and makes us feel as though we were going to be perpetually grounded. There is no other passage of such sustained prosaicness in his work after *Rienzi*, as the Herald makes his proclamations, the obedient chorus expresses its readiness to obey, the trumpet fanfares dutifully punctuating, the King summons the nobles to war, and then the first of the two villains, Friedrich von Telramund, delivers his lengthy accusation of Elsa, for black-magically removing her brother Gottfried. We are in the dark as to how this routine might conceivably connect with what we heard before the curtain went up. It is only with the arrival of Elsa and her attendants on the scene that the music changes its colours in a way that at least has some relation to the Prelude, if only through its purity and the delicacy of its scoring. Elsa clearly comes from another world, in the vulgar sense. She certainly is unable to make contact with the one she has appeared in, lost as she is in trance. When she finally begins, by an indirect route, to answer the King's questions, it is by narrating a dream, and in the middle of it, as, according to the stage direction, 'her expression changes from dreamy blissfulness to rapturous exaltation', we hear, though not in the original key, the theme of the Prelude, as she describes her knight in shining armour. The naturalness with which her characteristic motive, scored in pastel shades, and his, move into one another suggests that she, at any rate, can move in his world, the world of the Prelude, about whose significance we still have no information (that being the most significant thing about it).

There is a good deal more thumping and declaiming before Elsa's dream becomes reality, and then it is of an appropriately oneiric kind; Lohengrin arrives in his boat drawn by a swan. As he steps from his boat, the exalted tone of his thanks and farewell, almost unaccompanied as they are, leaves no doubt that he belongs to the realm, whatever it may be, of the Prelude. And the chorus, thus far bellicose and noisy, are so subdued by this vision of beauty that their expression of awe briefly takes them up onto the same plane. This is some of Wagner's loveliest music. Lohengrin obliges by coming down to their level, announcing his readiness to fight on Elsa's behalf in tones of combative energy. But if a singer with the right kind of voice is singing the name-part, his separateness from the stentorian baritones and basses who surround him will need no emphasis.

Once more we have a case, as with Senta and the Dutchman, where love at first sight proceeds from love at second sight. Lohengrin asks Elsa if she will marry him, granted that he is triumphant in vanquishing her accuser, but only on condition that she never asks him where he came from, or his name and provenance. This condition on their relationship is sung by Lohengrin to a phrase which, descending by an interval of a fifth, and then rising by steps, is a kind of tic of Wagner's, to be found in more or less this form in one opera after another, and almost always indicates some obstacle to love's fulfilment, or, as here, a warning about the end of love. Given the generally glowing nature of Lohengrin's music, it strikes an alarming note, though Elsa, in her dream of happiness, fails to register it.

What on earth, we may be wondering by this stage, is this opera about? It is all very well describing it as 'an exquisite lyrical picture in a heavy gilt frame', which does do justice to the way it presents itself, but the frame and the picture interact in a confusing way, and in any case what is it a picture of? What seems to be the most obvious answer is that it presents the world of political and at least incipient military action in realistic, if not naturalistic, terms: Friedrich von Telramund and his pagan consort Ortrud, the work's most powerful figure, are plausibly seen as politicians – indeed Wagner described them as that. Writing to Liszt in 1852, Wagner says, 'Ortrud is a woman who – *does not know love* ... Her nature is politics. A *male* politician disgusts us, a *female* politician appals us.' They are intriguers, liars, bent on power and unscrupulous in trying to attain it, prepared to use force if necessary. The King makes all the right noises for someone in control, talking of finding out the truth while actually believing that the strongest man is in the right. It may not be particularly interesting, but it is accurate. Can such a world – our world – be redeemed by the introduction of an idealistic figure from elsewhere, chivalrously coming to the rescue of someone who in her innocence is unequipped to deal with politicians?

I find that a convincing account, in brief, of the subject

of *Lohengrin*, and believe that it shows a striking advance in Wagner's art that he is prepared to tackle such a fundamental issue in operatic terms. But what we actually get from attending a performance of the work is a very different impression, and one which shows that Wagner, at this halfway point in his life, was facing his deepest crisis. In *Der fliegende Holländer* the ordinary folk serve only to set off in relief the seriousness of the central pair. In *Tannhäuser* the opposing poles of the Venusberg and the Wartburg are both undesirable, so it is only to be expected that Tannhäuser himself should panic-strickenly run from pillar to post. And, as we saw, Wagner loses his nerve in Act III and makes the only satisfactory person in the drama capitulate to the values of the Wartburg, and thereby redeem Tannhäuser, rendering the action incoherent. In *Lohengrin* he tries a new tack: the world of action and passion as we ordinarily know it is not simply to be rejected, but it has to be infused by value of a kind it is unacquainted with, and which it has to take on trust. Can we expect that, given its constituents, it will ever consent to do that? Or, in the first place, without considering the general run of people, will even such a romantic dreamer as Elsa agree to Lohengrin's terms, and should she?

Well, he does fight on her behalf with Telramund and win. So she has something solid to go on. The rest of the action consists essentially of Ortrud's planting seeds of doubt in her mind, and that leads to Elsa's turning her wedding night with Lohengrin into an increasingly urgent series of pleas that, if he really loves her, he should tell her what it is only natural that she wants to know. When he realises that he can't persuade her to desist, Lohengrin agrees to tell all, and to everyone, but only at the cost of returning whence he came, which leads to Elsa's death. At some point along the way what happens, surely, to every susceptible listener is that he abandons the conceptual structure of the action, and indulges himself in the gorgeous music which Wagner lavished on this strange plot – and lavished is the word. In no other of his works does he present us with such a bouquet of rich melody, sometimes scantily related to the action, as in the marvellous and enormous string tune which concludes the scene in which, in Act II, Ortrud succeeds in sowing suspicion in Elsa's mind. And the famous, or notorious, Prelude to Act III is the only piece of music in all Wagner's works which is thematically wholly unrelated to any of the rest of the work. It looks, or rather sounds, as if Wagner had lapsed into the cardinal sin of operatic composers, of allowing the drama to become the means to the end of music.

There are several reasons why *Lohengrin* was succeeded by five years during which Wagner wrote no more music, other than a few jottings for the *Ring*. But it is hard not to conclude that the basic one was that he realised that his musical genius and his dramatic concerns would, if he was not careful, grow apart, and he would become merely another operatic composer, even if one of extraordinary impressiveness. That is what he was determined not to be, and what he triumphantly didn't become. The test of an adequate performance of *Lohengrin* is that one wishes afterwards that Wagner had allowed himself the luxury of one more work of the same kind before he converted himself into a world-historical phenomenon, transforming attitudes and expectations on many fronts. The rapturous escapism of *Lohengrin* makes Elsas of us all, temporarily, dreaming of an existence which Malory put into prose and Tennyson, in *The Idylls of the King*, inadequately put into poetry.

So it soon becomes clear that close critical attention to the subject of *Lohengrin* is not going to be rewarding. Wagner's own writing about it, in his pivotal *A Communication to my*

Friends, is interesting in its own right, but also because it seems to intersect so little with our experience of the work. A straight reading of the text would lead anyone to think that, since Elsa only asks the forbidden question at Ortrud's instigation – and Ortrud is a superb villain – it is something that she clearly should not have done; and the consequences of her doing it are that the work ends more bleakly than any other in the Wagnerian canon. But Wagner's exegesis moves in a different direction: Lohengrin is, according to him, the character whose need is profoundest – Elsa needs him to get her out of a tough situation, but he needs her to 'become and to remain nothing other than a full and complete human being who would feel warm emotion and inspire it in another'. In other words he can't bear being who he is, with the isolation which that entails. But he wants things both ways: to feel 'warm emotion' and yet to be the recipient of it on terms that no one could sensibly expect to be fulfilled.

Surveying the scene, Wagner comes up with the stimulating and suggestive idea that what Lohengrin does not want to be is 'a god, i.e. an absolute artist'. This is, as Wagner is often inclined to be in prose, rather cryptic, especially since he fails to enlarge on it. But he may well have put his finger, at this moment, on a crucial issue which in some way he had to confront before he could proceed with the complete integrity that he always possessed in artistic matters. My conjecture is this: that Wagner had doubts which have been aired at intervals since Plato's dialogue the *Euthyphro*, about why we should do what the gods, or in the Christian era, God, commands. Is he (or He) to be worshipped simply on account of the fact that he is who he is, which is what orthodoxy has always inclined to? And if so, doesn't that make him (or Him) so unlike anyone else that it is hard for the concept of love to get a grasp? The gods, or God, get an enormous proportion of their prestige from being inscrutable, and thus they lead us, like Thurber's puzzled husband in the famous cartoon, to wonder what they want to be inscrutable for. They tempt us into the Ortrud-question: What do they have to hide? The answer that they have nothing to hide, but that they are testing our capacity for absolute trust, always seems evasive. And as soon as we say, as the unwise have often done for purposes of persuasion, that we have only to see how they behave to have a basis for trusting them, the 'absolute' element is abandoned; quite apart from the fact that there seems to be plenty going on around us which puts our trust under severe strain.

Supposing this is what Wagner had in mind in the *Communication*. The next aperçu, signalled by the 'i.e.', is that the 'absolute' artist is all too much like god in this worrying respect. For I take it that what Wagner means by 'the absolute artist' is a creator of works whose validity we have to accept, grateful for their beauty, and regarding any apparent faults in the works as incapacities on our part to appreciate the grand design. Yet the artist himself knows how much 'faking', to use E. M. Forster's word, went into the production of his works, and feels guilty at the extent to which we are gulled by his skill. He knows too, certainly if he has Wagner's boundless confidence in his own powers, and his understanding of their peculiar nature, to what extent he resembles Lohengrin, and thus transforms us, as I have said, into an audience of Elsas. It is therefore not surprising that Wagner produced this *prima facie* odd account of the opera, in which he claims that the real subject of the work is his own predicament. As the most intelligent and self-conscious, as well as the most intellectual of artists, he could see that in the Prelude he had written a new kind of music, one for which he had a dangerous gift: the music of hypnosis.

The music of *Lohengrin*, at any rate when it has to do with

Lohengrin himself, is the perfect realisation of its hero's demands: it too insists that it be accepted as the first and last word, or sound, because it is so beautiful. And the generally vastly lower level of the rest only enhances its power; to return to my earlier metaphor, it is a lyrical picture with an unappealingly incongruous frame. The exception to this is the music associated with the villains, but much more with Ortrud than her rather feeble side-kick Telramund. They dominate the Second Act, about which commentators who are more interested in what a given piece of Wagner's music leads to than what it is have often pointed out that the music which opens it, with its bizarre scoring and slithery chromatics, is a foretaste of the *Ring* which suggests that Wagner could have gone straight on to write it if he had chosen. And it does have the kind of gloomy power that we associate with Fafner, Alberich and some of the other sinister characters of the *Ring*. But the modes that Wagner was capable of in his masterworks, their variety and the smooth transitions between them, are not in the least degree indicated in *Lohengrin*. And the other great anti-heroic music in that act, Ortrud's invocation of the pagan gods, including 'Wodan' and 'Freia', is not innovative in idiom, even though its impact is a revelation of what conventional means can achieve. But though it is in vicious and ugly antithesis to the radiant silver-blue (about which almost everyone agrees) of Lohengrin's music, we are hardly likely to be seduced by it – as we might be by, say, some at least of Venus's music in *Tannhäuser*. Its effect, that is, is to make Lohengrin a still more alluring metaphysical matinée-idol.

So Wagner's dilemma remains. Even if we are not prone to take this opera all that seriously, we can understand, with a minimum of historical imagination, how it could have come to affect the young Ludwig II in the way that it did, giving him a lifelong conception of himself as the Swan King. So

Wagner was right to ponder the question of how to stop being an 'absolute artist' and become whatever the alternative to that is. He had, that is, to rehearse and relive for himself the celebrated Platonic anxieties about the effect of art, even if he seems to have been straining things somewhat in locating those anxieties in the figure of Lohengrin.

Quite apart from Wagner's profound musings on the subject, it is clear that *Lohengrin* represents a terminus. The other-worldly beauty and radiance of the Prelude are unable to engage with this world, and the attempt to make them can only result, as the work recognises, in tragedy or something like it (more like it than anything Wagner produced anywhere else). Wagner never wanted to be an aesthete, certainly not if art has beauty as a central feature. Art for him always had something to do with transforming consciousness, leaving no aspect of men's lives unchanged. He was a revolutionary in art because he wanted life and the world to be different, and he saw in the art of his time, above all in traditional opera, a reflection, all too faithful, of the world as it was. Instrumental music, on the other hand, even that composed by his idol Beethoven, is so far removed from what Hegel called 'the world's course' that it is likely to be seen as an alternative to existence. From that point of view, the harshest judgement one could pass on *Lohengrin* is that it succeeds in being both traditional opera and, in its effect, pure instrumental music – if the part of Lohengrin were ever to be sung ideally, he would sound more like an instrument than a voice. But for its composer that had its advantages. What better, if one is to make new resolutions and keep to them, than to have just done something that makes them not only desirable but imperative?

Yet, having just listened to *Lohengrin* again, this account that I have just given of it seems intolerably mean. It is not only the Prelude and the music associated with it which is beautiful, but also many passages in which, with uncharacteristic prodigality, Wagner pours out a great stream and never repeats it. That occurs not only in Act II, but also, for instance, after the main statement of the notorious Wedding March, where the strings seem eager to negate any hint of four-squareness. And the passage after the love duet has been brought to its peremptory conclusion, when Lohengrin wearily tells the servants to dress his bride – he is right in calling her that, but it is still a bitter irony – is almost unbearably poignant. Whatever its defects, and the right diagnosis of them, it is too lovely a work to live without.

7

Wagner Ponders

Wagner's theoretical writings, especially those he torrentially produced between 1849 and 1853, are usually thought, perhaps not always on the basis of extensive first-hand experience, to be windy, diffuse, abstract, confused, rambling and obscure. Unfortunately most of these charges are amply justified. Carl Dahlhaus, one of his best commentators, remarks that 'Wagner was an enthusiastic but impatient reader.' The same can be said of him as a writer. The impatience manifested itself, alas, in his trying to find out what he thought by writing until he had more or less exhausted the possibilities, but failing to go back and eliminate redundancies and contradictions. The result is that much of the finest reflection ever undertaken on the nature and importance of music-drama, and on many other subjects, goes unread.

Happily he was also a prolific letter-writer, and when he has a specific audience, his correspondent, in mind, he becomes much more lucid and direct, so that many valuable insights can be shared, and with great pleasure in the manner of their presentation, from reading selections of his correspondence. Even then, however, there often seems to be a gap between what was happening in his mind at a creative level and what he was able to express discursively – a good thing too, since otherwise it is quite possible that he would have exhausted himself in exegesis.

The bulk of the prose – he actually produced a stream of it

from his Paris days in 1839–1841 to the end of his life – was written in the years immediately subsequent to the abortive Dresden uprising of 1849, when Wagner, forced to flee Germany, settled in Zurich and wrote the poem of the *Ring*. He was driven to the realisation that the revolutions of 1848 and the next year were largely abortive because it was unclear to the revolutionaries what their long-term goals were. At the same time, as the *Ring* grew in scope and size from one music-drama to four, and Wagner saw that what he was doing was itself revolutionary in several ways, such that hopes for understanding it, or for its being adequately performed, were vain, he came to merge the two realisations: the *Ring* is about the corruption of present society, among other things, and thus of the greatest importance if a new innocence is to be found. But the corruption of consciousness of the members of society is so pervasive that they are not in a position to appreciate what the *Ring* is telling them; not, at any rate, without a great deal of preparatory explanation. Yet what he wanted, as we have seen at the beginning of this book, is that we should feel the truth of his message without damaging interference from the 'synthesising intellect'. His own restless intellect, second to none in its tireless synthesising, insisted on having many a protracted say, though he wasn't necessarily contravening his own edict. For he needed to explain to his potential audience what he conceived the highest significance of art to be – to point them in the right direction for witnessing his dramas.

That is why so much that Wagner wrote at this time was concerned with the nature of human society. The line that commentators customarily take is that what he was really interested in was his art and that alone, and that his speculations about the society of the future are really no more than propaganda on behalf of his endeavours, putting people in the right frame of mind for the demanding artistic experiences which he was going to vouchsafe them. To take him more seriously than that would be to indulge his megalomania, to fail to be embarrassed by what one ought to be embarrassed by. For what qualifications did Wagner have for thinking in an interesting or illuminating way on society?

The same questions, however, could be asked about many thinkers who are taken seriously on political and social matters. That Hegel propounded some ludicrous, even dangerous views about the Prussian state is only held to disqualify him from consideration on politics by readers who have not acquired the elementary wisdom that sense and folly can exist side by side in the most distinguished minds. I don't want to mount a full-scale reinstatement of Wagner as a discursive thinker here, because I am chiefly concerned to get clearer about the nature of what is his leading claim to enduring attention, and that is certainly his dramas. And I am not claiming that if he had not composed those astonishing works we would still be interested in him purely on account of his prose writings, although I am not sure that we shouldn't be. But I am claiming that it is a mistake to look patronisingly on them because it was a weird psychological necessity for him to sound off at length if he was to keep the didacticism out of his dramas. One might put it in this way: the specific points he had to make about life were to be made entirely in the dramas, and to be understood only by experiencing them. But the general point of writing them at all, and especially of writing something so drastically innovative, could not be made in them. If they were launched on the public without due explanation of their purpose they would be assimilated to other works in the operatic tradition, though they might be praised for their sustained inspiration or damned for their outrageous pretentiousness.

What Wagner feared has largely come to pass. His works

have joined the operatic repertoire, where they have no place. The limitless capacity of almost everyone for assimilating the strange and novel to what they already know has managed, even with him, to operate. Some anti-Wagnerians, naturally not very large a proportion, realise that and wonder what these extraordinary works are doing existing alongside those of Mozart, Verdi, Puccini and Richard Strauss. Their hostility registers their awareness that he is out of place in their company – though that need not entail a value-judgement.

But he was no better served by those – now, I suspect, extinct – who took his prose works as the systematic statement of a new world-view, and lived according to its dictates. In fact their selection of texts was, as always in such cases, gratifying to what they already wanted to think. And what they took more notice of than the writings, which were in any case constantly evolving as Wagner, always susceptible to new ideas, embraced one theory after another, were some of his least savoury opinions, aired in the *ex cathedra* manner which Cosima encouraged in the last decade and a half of his life. They then sat through the music-dramas in what seems to have been a coma induced by treating them as ritual, and emerged more complacent than when they went in. That kind of thing was most manifest in what was known in the early years of this century as the 'Bayreuth Circle'. There is as much point in blaming Wagner for it as there is in blaming Christ for the Spanish Inquisition.

There are two areas where it is particularly important to get Wagner's ideas as clear as their nature permits, and then at last we are free to move on to the works which would demand and repay attention. The first I have already said a little about, and don't need to add much more. At the time when he was thinking along his new lines, a few months after his flight from Dresden, he wrote to his friend Ferdinand

Heine (no relation of Heinrich): 'All hopes which are directed towards a long artistic life rest basically upon the uncreative poverty of mankind: if men were as they ought to be, a work of art would flourish today and die tomorrow, leaving a new one in its place in full fresh bloom.' The trope of the work of art as being, or being like, a living organism is of course a familiar one. But the concentration has usually been on the relationship of its parts to one another, a contrast with the mechanical, and so forth. It was rare for a Romantic to take the image to the point where he not only admitted, but also wished, that successive works would die and be replaced by others. For Wagner, a work of art would have served its purpose when it had been an instrument in the advance of man, and he even went so far as to envisage a time when there would no longer be a necessity for art at all – when everyone lived a boundlessly creative life. More than two years later he wrote to Theodor Uhlig: 'My dear friend! I am often now beset by strange thoughts about "art", and on the whole I cannot help feeling that, if we had *life*, we should have no need of *art*. Art begins at precisely the point where life breaks off: where nothing more is present, we call out in art, "I wish". I simply do not understand how a *truly happy* individual could ever hit upon the idea of producing "art": only in life can we "achieve" anything – is our "art" therefore not simply a confession of our impotence?' Wildly utopian, no doubt, but hardly an overestimate of the eternal value of his own works. Not surprisingly, the more pessimistic he became about mankind's advance, then or ever, the more protective about the survival of his works he became too, and quite logically.

Less than a year after the first letter I quoted, when his conception of the *Ring* had developed somewhat, Wagner wrote to another friend, Ernst Kietz, about how he thought of its being performed: 'According to this plan of mine, I would have a theatre erected here [in Zurich] on the spot, made of planks, and have the most suitable singers join me here, and arrange everything necessary for this one special occasion, so that I could be certain of an outstanding performance of the opera. I would then send out invitations far and wide to all who were interested in my work, ensure that the auditorium was decently filled, and give three performances – free, of course – one after the other in the space of a week [Wagner still was thinking of only one opera, *Siegfrieds Tod*], after which the theatre would then be demolished and the whole affair would be over and done with.' Extravagant notions of this kind came naturally to Wagner, and it may be comforting to find them mad. But though the mind boggles at the idea of such a conflagration, it registers the point that once Wagner's art had had its effect he saw no further purpose for it. But it never did have the effect he wanted it to. His whole view of art was at the opposite pole from Kant's devastatingly harmful idea of will-less contemplation.

Things rapidly became more complicated. Two years after his major theatrical efforts, he discovered, thanks to another friend, the philosophy of Schopenhauer, and, as with so many other artists of the latter half of the nineteenth century, it struck him with the force of revelation, and one to which he remained, after his own fashion, true to the end of his life. The chief effects were twofold: in the first place, as soon as he read a pessimistic philosopher (they are hard to find) he felt that he had come across someone who had put into words what he had long felt, though one might not have guessed it from the basic idea of the *Ring*, which was that the rule of law of the gods should be replaced by a society in which human beings were governed by the love they felt for one another. The failure of the revolutions certainly contributed to a more sombre outlook, but that hadn't been enough to discourage him from going ahead with the *Ring* poem, and beginning to set it, finally, to music.

The second way in which Schopenhauer made Wagner alter at least his official views was in his attitude to music. His position as worked out most fully in *Opera and Drama* was that music was to play a subordinate role – the famous means-end formula, drama being the end. Schopenhauer, uniquely in the history of Western philosophy, not only considered music at length, but gave it the supreme place among the arts and awarded it a super-cognitive role. His view of the world as Will, in its essential nature, left him with the question of how art can depict that in the most direct way. Schopenhauer argues that the arts other than music are concerned with the apparent world, or the world in which the Will is manifested in acts of will in the ordinary sense; but they are unable to reach the underlying reality itself. Music, by being non-conceptual, is able to portray the Will itself in operation, or even, he sometimes claims, is the Will. Since the Will is given a negative value, it remains unclear, to put it gently, why we derive such satisfaction from listening to music – presumably Schopenhauer is here labouring, as his disciple (for a short period) Nietzsche also did, from the long-held view of philosophers that there is a peculiar satisfaction in knowing the truth about things, whatever it may be. One might have thought that ignorance was bliss, but Schopenhauer was wholly unconvinced about the possibility of bliss, so all that remained was to take a grim consolation from being aware of how bad things really are.

The notion that music is the hotline to ultimate truth is one that almost any composer would be likely to find attractive, especially since it is so hard to account for the extraordinary power of music in any ordinary conceptual scheme. Wagner had only to read Schopenhauer's views on music to be instantly persuaded, the more so since they were all of a piece with the philosophy of pessimism; and since Wagner was afflicted with an excess of will – one proposition about him that is uncontroversial – the idea of the Will's appeasement as being the road to salvation was one which not only told him what he wanted to hear about himself, but also enabled him to make retrospective sense of his operas to date. Writing to Liszt, now his closest friend, to announce his conversion to Schopenhauer, he virtually identifies himself with his own Flying Dutchman: 'When I think back to the storms that have buffeted my heart and on its convulsive efforts to cling to some hope in life – against my own better judgement –, indeed, now that these storms have swelled so often to the fury of a tempest,– I have yet found a sedative which has finally helped me to sleep at night; it is the sincere and heartfelt yearning for death: total unconsciousness, complete annihilation, the end of all dreams – the only ultimate redemption!'

It is easy to dismiss Wagner's frequent claims in his correspondence that he is only waiting for death, that his nerves are so shattered that he can't go on much longer, and so forth, as typically Romantic, and especially typically Wagnerian, posturing, part of the 'actor' which Nietzsche said was so large a part of his personality. But they seem to me perfectly consonant with his insatiable appetite for life, just as suicide is often a manifestation of frustrated vitality. Wagner, like many of his central dramatic figures, was intent on life going his way to an extent which may be seen as childish or heroic. Seeing it as childish seems to me too easy, if only because we aren't as clear as we might be on the concept of the childish itself. Not that we have yet got clear about the concept of the heroic, but that is the direction in which I am moving.

For we need to explain a crux in Wagner's life and art which may be the most puzzling of all, and which has been oddly ignored by writers on him. His position in 1854, when he made his discovery of Schopenhauer, was this: he had written, in reverse order, the whole poem of the *Ring*, had set the 'preliminary evening', as he insisted on calling *Das Rheingold* in order to keep the complete work as a trilogy, and was still composing *Die Walküre*, with the whole of *Siegfried* and *Götterdämmerung* ahead. One might have expected that he would be stopped dead in his tracks by Schopenhauer, for whatever the final import of the *Ring* might be, it simply cannot be construed as being as pessimistic as it should be if Schopenhauer's philosophy were correct. So why did Wagner continue to compose it, admittedly with drastic changes to the very end of the cycle? It would have been absurdly superficial of him to entertain, and it would be absurdly superficial of us to attribute to him, the notion that altering the last five minutes of the work could alter the impact of the whole.

An alternative explanation, but no more satisfactory, is that, Macbeth-like, he had waded in so far that he could only go on. Though Wagner never abandoned a drama which he had in part composed, it seems to me that he would have been prepared to do even that if he felt that it was sufficiently at odds with his *Weltanschauung*. What seems to be most plausible is that he felt the text and the action were sufficiently indeterminate for the music, which thanks to Schopenhauer now took a more commanding role, to take the responsibility for what the work came to mean. That is certainly consistent with his frequent injunctions to correspondents to wait until they *heard* the *Ring*. There are even times when it seems as if Wagner himself waited for the music to tell him what he meant, and when he claimed that he was in no better a position, having composed it, than anyone else to say what it meant. In other words, he trusted his artistic impulses, coming from a level of his personality to which he did not have full access, while at the same time he was unable to turn down opportunities to explain it. What he knew was that in the *Ring* he had presented a set of characters, and an action, which were sufficiently rich to be all that he needed for understanding and changing the world. What, it appears, he did not know was what the relationships between the innumerable elements in the vast structure were. To grasp that was the responsibility of feeling, not of the 'synthesising intellect'. We shall see.

There is a further basic issue which needs airing, if not coping with, before we move on to the rest of his works, since it is something that all of them are more or less obsessed by. But it is in the *Ring* in particular that Wagner deals with it, and that is at least in part responsible for the degree of fascination that the *Ring* continues to generate. The issue is the relationship of the individual to society. What do we need, if anything, in terms of a social context, for our deepest and most peremptory urgings (they are always the same in Wagner, marking a sharp distinction between him and any form of 'realist' art) to be satisfied? Could one realise what matters most in isolation from society? And if not, what are the conditions that the society needs to possess for the individual's fulfilment? Once more we see how Wagner was driven to do a lot of troubled thinking after *Lohengrin*, in which the hero is both needed by a society and needs it, but there are no terms in which the connection between them can be worked out, so he simply returns to Montsalvat, and it doesn't look as if anything is going to be different in Antwerp, where the action of the opera takes place, or that Lohengrin has learned anything except to be more cautious before he next answers a cry of distress.

Yet Wagner's reading of, and agreement in some form with, Schopenhauer meant that in the last resort questions of politics and social relationships, like questions of history, became comparatively superficial for him. For Schopenhauer's metaphysics of the Will make anything that happens in the phenomenal world, the world that we see, feel and act in, finally insignificant. Even – and this may be his profoundest influence on Wagner – the belief that there are separate individuals is one that applies only to phenomena. The underlying Will is one, and Schopenhauer ascribes many of the evils of life to our illusion of 'the principle of individuation'. We think that we are selves, but that is our worst mistake. For at the merely ethical level it leads to egoism and malice, the first being the illusion that we can thrive at the expense of other people, the second that we can hurt other people without hurting ourselves. The sole basis of morality, according to Schopenhauer, is compassion, which springs from the awareness that I am my neighbour, in the most literal sense, and therefore that we should stop thinking in terms of me helping my neighbour, except as a risky figure of speech. When I do good to someone else, which can only consist (again according to Schopenhauer's bleak view) in alleviating his pain, I am equally doing good to myself. One might retort that when I am doing good to myself, I am really doing it equally to others, but that is not a point that Schopenhauer or his disciples ever make.

Details aside, one can get a general image of the way Schopenhauer sees the world, and it is best to stop there, since his metaphysics soon becomes incoherent. But it is easy to understand why he has had such an appeal, at least to non-philosophers who feel that the world is a bad place and that the root of the trouble is somehow closely involved with the isolation of people. But the isolation being of an emphatically metaphysical kind, beyond the grasp of the senses or even of reason as ordinarily understood, programmes of social reform are quite beside the point. It is just as foolish to think that replacing capitalism by socialism would improve matters – the

superficiality of the revolutions of 1848 infuriated Schopenhauer. His concession to our ordinary awareness of the world
is to advocate compassion; but that *is* a concession. At the level
that really matters, where there is no individuality, we can
only appease the Will by contemplation and disinterested
knowledge, though it is not clear how they do the trick.

But once again, if we leave the difficulties aside, we can see
that Schopenhauer is committed to the view that each person
has to achieve his own salvation by negating his own will,
finally by realising that there is not a genuine 'he' to be counted
among the items in ultimate reality. Social relations are of no
interest, except to the connoisseur of human folly, and sexual
relations in particular are objectionable, deluding us into
thinking that life is worth living, spawning more delusory
individuals, and often being paradigmatic assertions of will.

We find, then, that long before Nietzsche, Barthes, Derrida,
Foucault and their innumerable progeny came along,
Schopenhauer had 'decentred' the self with a vengeance. He
would not have taken sides in the contemporary disputes of
cultural materialists versus essentialist humanists, or post-
structuralists versus everyone who has preceded them. Since
there are no selves, centred or otherwise, these people are all
wasting their breath, partly because they think that they are
arguing against other people. And Wagner would probably
have agreed. But, as is the way with artists, Wagner was more
tolerant of appearances than Schopenhauer was. In the end,
as we shall see when we come to *Die Meistersinger*, Wagner
achieved a wisdom about the relationship between appearance
and reality which has eluded philosophers, who all, if they
subscribe to the dichotomy, have masochistically, perhaps
sadistically too, been determined that we abandon our lifelong
addiction to appearance, even though they can never tell us
how to do it.

The chief point of this digression, as it must have seemed, is to indicate that Wagner put himself into a strange position by converting to Schopenhauerianism in the middle of creating the *Ring*, for that work is crucially concerned to show how we might move from a law-governed to a love-governed society, as I have said. Yet in the end the prospects for any society whatever are null, which may be the point of the revised ending of the work. So immediately, before we look at it in any detail, it is worth mentioning that Wagner's celebrated twelve-year gap in composing the *Ring*, between Acts II and III of *Siegfried*, was devoted artistically to creating one work, *Tristan und Isolde*, in which the lovers explicitly reject the values of human society and the notion of selfhood, and another, *Die Meistersinger von Nürnberg*, in which the central character, Hans Sachs, devotes himself, when he is not being a cobbler or poet, to understanding how illusion can be coped with, since it can't be conquered.

8

What is the *Ring* About?

Whatever else people disagree on concerning the meaning of the *Ring*, there seems to be unanimity that it is about the conflict between Love and Power. In the opening scene of *Das Rheingold* Wellgunde says, 'Der Welt Erbe gewänne zu eigen, wer aus dem Rheingold schüfe den Ring, der maasslose Macht ihm verlieh'' (The inheritance of the world would be won by him who made the Ring from the Rhinegold, it would vouchsafe him limitless power); and at the beginning of his monologue in Act II of *Die Walküre*, as Wotan lays bare his soul to Brünnhilde, he says, 'Als junger Liebe Lust mir verblich, verlangte nach Macht mein Muth' (When the joy of young love departed from me, my spirit longed for power). Alberich, whom Wellgunde unwisely tells about the power of the Ring, forthwith renounces love and thereby gets the action of the whole drama under way (at least, that is what we think at that stage, unaware of anything that has happened previously), putting the gods and giants whom we encounter in the next scene into a state of anxiety about being under Alberich's power. And Wotan says he won the world for himself. A parallel is immediately established between the two, and since Wotan is the major presence in the *Ring*, and Alberich its chief villain, it does look as if their giving up love for power provides the essential dynamic of the whole work.

We need to press the issue a bit harder, however, before we agree to this simple-to-grasp mnemonic. Recall, or play, the opening scene of *Das Rheingold*. After the Prelude has evoked the primeval depths of the Rhine for us – but note that it does more than that: it begins statically, though the Rhine itself is in perpetual motion, and the first motif we hear is as much that of 'Werden' (becoming) as of the Rhine itself – we have the Rhinemaidens, carefree and frivolous creatures of the deep, singing their nature-song and playing their immemorial games. As soon as Alberich emerges from a dark gully, they begin their merciless prick-teasing, and continue with it until the Gold begins to glow. It is then that they inform Alberich about what could be done by someone who stole the Gold and made the Ring out of it, and the first shadow falls over the music, to chilling effect, as Woglinde says 'Nur wer der Minne Macht versagt . . .' (Only he who forswears love . . .). Alberich promptly does so, tearing the Gold from the rock as he curses love.

What, though, is the love which Alberich curses and forswears? It is not being priggish to say that he is merely in lust, and certainly not a criticism of him; the Rhinemaidens could hardly, in their simplicity, be an object of anything more. And they surely deserve the punishment that Alberich deals them, having comprehensively insulted him as well as flirted, with the unconscious cruelty of children. What they represent is amoral nature, no more to be praised or condemned than Alberich. The criteria in operation here are aesthetic: the Rhinemaidens are lovely, Alberich is ugly. Since he is prepared to sacrifice 'love' he is also to a degree heroic. The gods speak about him in severely moralistic terms, but that gives us no reason to agree with them, the less in that they are all acting out of self-interest. The character whom the Alberich of the opening scene most resembles is Fasolt, the entirely sympathetic giant who undertook to collaborate with his boorish brother Fafner to build Valhalla because he wants some beauty, in the form of Freia, in his life. And he tellingly says to Wotan, when he realises that the god doesn't intend to keep his word, 'Die ihr durch Schönheit herrscht, schimmernd hehres Geschlecht' (You who rule through beauty, you augustly glittering race), showing once more – and surely Wagner's sympathies are with him, as they are with Alberich until he turns nasty – that what is ugly or coarse ('Wir Plumpen plagen uns' – We thickheads toil away – says Fasolt) yearns to enhance its existence through contact with beauty. Where Alberich meets with the Rhinemaidens' giggling contempt, Fasolt has to endure Wotan's insufferable self-righteousness, as if the gods have a monopoly on beauty. Wagner is here portraying a world which doesn't yet have sophisticated or perhaps even coherent concepts of power and love.

Wagner called *Das Rheingold* 'a preliminary evening' to the *Ring*, and it is, in many obvious ways, very different from anything that follows. It is, for one thing, action-packed in a way no other of his works is. But it is also argument-packed, and has a remarkable number of articulate characters. Since Wagner wrote the text last, after those of the three succeeding dramas, he can have been in no doubt as to what it was preliminary to. But he wrote the music to it first, and it is widely agreed that in it he is more faithful than he is anywhere else to the doctrine of *Opera and Drama* that the music is only a means for articulating the drama. So it is not surprising that *Das Rheingold* has a different feel to the rest of the *Ring*. During most of the passages where discussion is taking place, the orchestra is quiet, and the rate at which the text is got through is much faster than in any other of Wagner's works, with the exception of parts of *Die Meistersinger* (which is an exception to everything). But it is more different from what succeeds it than any of that would lead one to expect.

The atmosphere of *Das Rheingold* is a chilly and chilling

one. Love, or what is called love in it, is renounced early on, but the only love-music we hear is the parody produced by the Rhinemaidens, which out of context would be very serviceable for a seduction. The way in which, after they do their flirting, they send up Alberich's passionate responses, is almost as disconcerting for us as it is for him. And the only other, this time genuinely, tender music in *Das Rheingold* is that of Fasolt, which earns him his brother's and Wotan's ridicule.

As is well known, the reason Wagner wrote four dramas instead of one was that he felt the first (i.e. the last), then the penultimate, then the antepenultimate, parts of the *Ring* were too burdened with explanation and narration, which held up the action. But he failed to remove the admittedly large quantities of explanation, sometimes even increasing them. He realised that they were in fact not rendered superfluous, so it follows that *Das Rheingold* fulfils some function other than enabling the subsequent dramas to stick to action. And – a quite separate point – Wagner can have had no idea when he composed the music for *Das Rheingold* of how he was going to develop as a composer, more especially as a result of the twelve-year gap between Acts II and III of *Siegfried*. But it is also amazing to watch his progress in the course of *Das Rheingold* itself, which becomes more sophisticated and elaborate by the minute. Clearly he was eager, when he decided to have his preliminary evening, to rise to the challenge of depicting rather than merely describing the primal scene. But what he can't have known was that the means at his disposal were relatively speaking primitive too. To say that they serve their purpose is insulting with faint praise. But the opening scene of *Götterdämmerung*, in which the three Norns recall what occurred – as it happens, what occurred in large part before the events of *Das Rheingold* – shows how immeasurably Wagner advanced in his sophisticated evocation of origins.

The relatively simple music of *Das Rheingold* is well suited to the expository function of the work, then, but in its starkness, which is especially noticeable if one is familiar with the rest of the *Ring*, it conveys a certain emotional tone. There are only two extended passages where Wagner allows a character to expand on an emotion, and it is extraordinary how much more powerful one is than the other. They are Loge's account, in Scene 2, of the omnipresence of Love; and Alberich's plans for world-domination, expressed to Wotan and Loge in Scene 3. These passages are clearly meant to be symmetrical, so may seem to add weight to the Love versus Power view of the work. But if one examines them with any care, there can be no question of which of the two carries more conviction.

Loge, the *Ring*'s ironist, makes a, for Wotan, tardy appearance – as the god of deceit as well as fire, his services are sorely needed to get Wotan out of his promise to the giants. He tells Wotan that what has been delaying him has been his worldwide search for a substitute for Freia, but that wherever he looked, he found that no one thought the 'delight and value' of woman was replaceable. At this, 'all express astonishment and consternation', reads the strange stage direction – it is hard to know whether Wagner or the characters are being naïve. Loge then launches into his account of his quest for 'was wohl dem Manne mächt'ger dünk, als Weibes Wonne und Werth' (what man might deem mightier than woman's delights and worth). The accompaniment to all this is fuller than anything else we have heard so far, self-consciously lush, making elaborate use of a motif associated with Freia and therefore with love. But there is something suspect about it, especially in relation to the character who is singing. This is love seen very much from the outside, and without any suggestion of any feeling other than physical desire. Loge is standing aside, even more than usual, from the company he keeps. And it becomes obvious that he is building up to something: it turns out to be an account of what we witnessed in Scene 1, Alberich's robbery of the Gold; and this in turn leads up to Loge's telling the assembled company that he had promised the complaining Rhinemaidens that he would get Wotan to engineer the return of the Gold to the Rhine. By now he is being openly malicious, as Wotan snaps with annoyance. In fact it is only a moment before Wotan is beginning to wonder how he might get the Gold from Alberich for himself, or preferably the Gold made into the Ring. Nothing easier, says Loge: just renounce love. Wotan once more reacts peevishly, and then says – a key moment: 'Den Ring muss ich haben!' (I must have the Ring!).

By this stage it has become plain that though the consequences of forswearing love are heavy, the thing itself is a tool in the power-struggle. Love – desire and possession – is just a, or possibly the major, way in which people (including mermaids, dwarves and gods) manipulate one another. At least, that is what it is in the frigid world of *Das Rheingold*. Love as caring, affection, warmth, tenderness or passion is a glaring absence. It rather seems, at this stage, that if love is going to play a leading role in the *Ring*, it is something that will come into being when all concerned, including Wotan, have had experiences of a kind that necessitate it, as they manifestly have not to date. The goddess of love and youth herself, Freia, is such a cypher in the action, so much merely a matter of who has her so that she can perform her function as a permanent face-lifter, or decoration of their existence, that it is astonishing that she should be thought to be of intrinsic interest – that is, that love might be valued as something more than a strategic weapon. This is a world in which everyone is waiting, but as yet they have no idea what they are waiting for.

Now look at the other extended expression of an emotion.

Wotan and Loge have descended to Nibelheim, the mine where Alberich has the Nibelungs toiling ceaselessly to get him ever more gold, and where his brother Mime, the craftiest smith, has special responsibilities to make Alberich his Tarnhelm, which enables him to change his shape at will, and to make the Ring itself from the Rhinegold. The intensity of this scene, in relation to anything which has gone before, is awe-inspiring. After a conversation with Mime, in which the wretched dwarf explains his woes to the visitors – to be answered only by their mirth – Alberich himself appears, and is justifiably suspicious of their presence. Wotan replies grandly, Loge with his usual sarcasm. But when Alberich says, 'die ganze Welt gewinn' ich mit ihm mir zu eigen' (I shall win the whole world with [the gold]), Wotan's pseudo-courteous reply conceals his unease, as he asks Alberich how he intends to set about his world-winning task. Alberich's reply is cunningly (by Wagner) constructed: he begins by evoking the carefree, enchanted existence of the gods, moving swiftly to a prophecy of its destruction: first Wotan's male companions will be brought low, then Alberich will have his way with their women, even if he doesn't have their love (whatever that may be). The whole passage builds up with frightening power, with a loathsome version of the Freia motif on a solo violin, suggestive of how perverted Alberich's lust has now become; and it climaxes in his manic laughter at the imminent realisation of his plans. Wotan is furious, but he must also be very anxious. Only thanks to Alberich's hubris and Loge's cunning does he manage to regain control of the situation, and finally, after the three of them have ascended back to the rocky heights of Scene 2, Alberich bound hand and foot, to get the Ring itself, by violence.

The scene in which Wotan divests Alberich of one after another of his possessions, much to Alberich's justified rage, though he knows he needn't worry so long as he keeps the Ring, is painful enough. But Wotan's demand, finally, for the Ring itself, and Alberich's agonised response, 'Das Leben, doch nicht den Ring!' (My life, but not the Ring!), to which Wotan 'forcefully' replies, 'Den Reif verlang ich: mit dem Leben mach, was du willst' (I demand the Ring: do what you like with your life), is, so long as Wotan has not been made, by a producer, into an absurd and degenerate delinquent from his first appearance, one of the most powerfully hideous passages in world drama.

Taking their cue from this passage above all, recent productions of the *Ring* have portrayed Wotan from the start as merely decrepit, morally and even physically. Not only does Wagner not need underlining in this way, but it is essential to the balance of the whole trilogy that, despite his capacity for treachery, violence and self-deceit, there is still genuine nobility in Wotan. He is, among other things, a politician, with all the vileness that entails. But Wagner is also concerned that he should be seen as a visionary, and Valhalla, as the wonderful theme which designates it reveals, is a conception far removed from anything Albert Speer might have dreamt up. Is it asking too much of contemporary audiences to contemplate a larger-than-life character who has virtues and vices on an equally extreme scale? Apparently producers feel that it is. The result is that Wotan appears, in *Das Rheingold*, as nothing more than a politician, and Valhalla is downgraded to Wall Street, or some similarly debased underpinning of late capitalism. Furthermore, it means that the Wotan we meet in Act II of *Die Walküre* is to all intents and purposes a different person. Remembering that Wagner composed the text of the *Ring* backwards, he portrayed his Wotan in *Das Rheingold* in the light of the figure whom he had already fully worked out in the subsequent two dramas. Given the fate which overtakes him at the end of the cycle, it is clear that he had to have done something adequately appalling in *Das Rheingold*, and that he be depicted as someone who is convincingly capable of that; but that it never be forgotten that he is the head of the gods, that he harbours aspirations for using his power benignly, and that he is awarded much of the grandest, noblest music in the cycle.

I wouldn't stress these obvious points at such solemn length if they weren't in danger of being completely overlooked. But if they are, then the *Ring* becomes something in which one can take only a picaresque interest, and I take it that we should employ the principle of critical charity, making works as coherent as we plausibly can. What I think tends to happen is that many people do regard Wotan as two characters, one the trickster of *Das Rheingold*, the other the tormented and introverted god, a much more 'modern' figure, of Acts II and III of *Die Walküre*, and of course still more depressed as the Wanderer in *Siegfried*. That he has become older, sadder, certainly an aspirer after wisdom, is undeniable. In *Das Rheingold* he is still trying out the limits of his power, and is not the least scrupulous in doing so. By the end, after Erda's warning, he is already chastened, as he is not by the tremendous force of Alberich's curse on the Ring. That leaves him cold, so intoxicated is he with being its possessor. After Alberich's departure, and after Wagner has given him some of the *Ring*'s most portentous music, Wotan merely remarks, 'Gönn ihm die geifende Lust!' (Let him have his bilious pleasure!), lost as he is in contemplation of the Ring. There follow eleven bars of the work's most quietly radiant music, as the higher strings clear the air, and it does temporarily seem as if hope has returned to the world. And the mood of optimism continues as the other gods return. This brief but lovely passage seems to vouchsafe a view of the kind of world that Wotan wants to rule over, and at least for its opening stretch it is thematically unrelated to anything else in the *Ring*, suggesting that we are being shown things 'objectively', at any rate not from an interested point of view.

Is it a piece of special pleading on Wagner's part? If we take the standard contemporary view of Wotan, it evidently is. If we don't, then it unassertively (many of Wagner's major points are made quietly) does postulate what everyone sometimes entertains the possibility of: a new start, the slate wiped clean. Wagner puts us into that state of mind, before scrupulously showing us that it can't be so. No warnings from anyone else have had any effect on Wotan, so when it comes to the ultimate crunch, the giants demanding the Ring to eliminate all possibility of seeing Freia, Wotan determined, naturally, to hold onto it, it is only the cryptic appearance of Erda, who sees everything that was, is and will be, which persuades him to relinquish it. She also produces what has always been seen as *the* riddle of the *Ring*: to music of intense gravity, she warns that everything that is will end, and that the gods are doomed, it seems, in any case. So what is the motive for Wotan to give up the Ring if he can't, even by doing that, save the situation? Whatever the answer, that conundrum lies at the heart of the *Ring*. Meanwhile, Alberich's curse comes into action with terrifying promptness. Having been given the Ring, Fasolt and Fafner immediately quarrel over its ownership, and Fasolt is butchered by his brother. Wotan is horrified, and it is only Donner's dispersal of the clouds that leads to the full view of Valhalla, and a brief remission of Wotan's anxiety, before he again wonders how things might turn out.

The entry of the gods into Valhalla, even then, is spoiled for them by the Rhinemaidens lamenting their lost Gold. Loge makes a final cynical jest, to the effect that they don't need it since they have the gods' glory to bask in, and then they all – except Loge, the ironical moralist, who disdains to join them – proceed grandly over the Rainbow Bridge, to the accompaniment of music both grand and grandiose: there is no doubt of the hollowness at the heart of Wotan's great scheme.

The unblinking honesty that pervades *Das Rheingold* is something to marvel at. Wagner has depicted a primal world which is corrupt from the start, thus producing something at odds with the central myth of Western culture. Power and libido are what animates it, together with a strong sense of natural beauty, which alone seems to offer any joy, at this stage. The only thing which almost all the characters have in common is awe in the presence of the aesthetic: the Rhinemaidens halted in their teasing of Alberich by the radiance of their Gold, Alberich bewitched by their loveliness, Fasolt spellbound by Freia, the gods placing a supreme premium on the beauty of youthfulness. And the score, which faithfully mirrors and comments on the trickeries and viciousness of so much of the action, still manages to create a sense of wonder in the listener at the magnificence of the setting in which all this moral squalor occurs, heightens it by the contrast. At the end one is left, almost, wishing that consciousness would disappear and leave what, actually, would be pointless without it. At the same time, there are enough suggestions in the text that we have not yet exhausted the possibilities of conscious life, and so we end this 'preliminary evening' with the paradoxical sense that we have begun by learning the worst, and that there is in this work a realism which depicts our world, despite the fact that no human beings have yet arrived on the scene. So if there is to be hope, it will come with their arrival – exactly the opposite to what one might have expected. It takes a very unusual artist to order things this way round.

9

Men and Gods

Die Walküre begins with a storm, but unlike the one which Donner had used to clear the sultry atmosphere towards the end of *Das Rheingold* this is a harrying, battering storm which leads the first human being we have encountered in the *Ring* to find shelter in a hut built round an ash tree. Once the elements have subsided, the music traces his exhaustion, as he collapses on the hut's floor. The noise disturbs a woman, and she comes in to see who the stranger might be.

The first thing that strikes us about this music, apart from its warm expressiveness, is its tentativeness. These are people lost, bewildered in the face of what life is doing to them. The contrast with *Das Rheingold* is instantly established. There, though issues became rapidly obscure, everyone's feelings were clear. Among those primitives, the idea of self-knowledge could gain no purchase, because no one had any doubts about how they felt and what they wanted. Hence the hard-edged quality of that work, the sharpness of the conflicts, and the unforgiving nature of its impact. Hence, too, its incomplete character. Its ending is a carefully false one, undermined by its own assertiveness; and, recalling Wagner's formulation about our feelings being put at rest, we realise that they have hardly been awoken yet. We have been – and the more one gets to know *Das Rheingold*, the truer it becomes – fascinated but rarely moved. As soon as *Die Walküre* begins we are moved by the helplessness of two people of whose origins we as yet know nothing. The man is quickly established as a wounded hero, the woman as an unhappy wife, longing to express a tenderness that she normally isn't permitted. When she brings the man a drink of mead, and they share it, a long melody for solo 'cello brings a depth and intensity of longing into the work which, even on first hearing, make an unforgettable impression.

The First Act of *Die Walküre* has a sureness of touch and a perfection of structure which puts it into a different class from anything which Wagner had previously attempted or achieved. It delineates, as had never been done before in drama, the gradual but inevitable growth of passion from anxiety and sympathy. That takes place in the text and the action, but still more so in the orchestra, now allotted a much more central role than it had had in *Das Rheingold*. There are very many long stretches in Act I, in particular, during which no one speaks, but their feelings develop and change, charted with uncanny mastery by the orchestra. That is partly because, despite the mutual sympathy of Siegmund and Sieglinde (we only learn their names in the closing minutes of the Act, Hunding having insisted on his from the outset), they are both, in the light of their wretched lives, too nervous to give away anything that they don't have to, and for them, as for so many epic figures, to let people know one's name is to give them a power over one. Oral communication, until Sieglinde has drugged Hunding to make sure he doesn't disturb them, is kept to immediate, practical purposes. Siegmund tells the married pair his history, though under an assumed name, and concealing his parentage, under duress. It is only when Hunding is safely asleep, and Sieglinde is acting from the conviction that the man who can pull the sword from the tree has at last arrived, that they urgently tell one another as much as possible, though still being cagey about their true origins

– life has taught them the harshest lessons, and trust, even between people with an immediate sympathetic bond, is only slowly established.

Characteristically, once the door has swung open to admit the spring moonlight, Siegmund is intent on lyrical outpourings, while it is Sieglinde who wants to move things along, to find out who he really is, who his father was, what is the source of the overpowering attraction which they feel for one another. I mean that that is characteristic of Wagner's men and women – the woman leads the way, the man rhapsodises. But what both are doing equally is discovering their feelings. When Siegmund launches into his Spring Song, it begins (to the reproaches of many commentators) as an aria about winter being vanquished; but before he has got far into it, he abandons the regular form in which he has begun, and moves into a premonitory image of spring being lured by Love, so that the 'sister-bride' is freed by her brother – all this before they discover that they are the Wälsung twins. Rapture contained in metrical form gives place to determination unconstrained, and the move from one to the other gives an immense release of energy, taken over at its climax: 'vereint sind Liebe und Lenz!' (Spring and Love are made one!), by Sieglinde telling 'Wehwalt' (Woeful), as she still pretends to think Siegmund is called, 'Du bist der Lenz, nach dem ich verlangte' (You are the spring for which I longed). They move, inexorably thanks to Sieglinde, to their moment of recognition, when Siegmund's admission that his father was Wälse (as he knew Wotan) leads to Sieglinde's ecstatic naming of him, giving him the will and energy to pull the sword Nothung from the tree.

This Act is so surely constructed, so full of warmth, and so moving in its progression from darkness and despair to love and light, that it is the one to play to anybody who doesn't know Wagner, and wants to find out what is so extraordinary about him. Amazing as the movement from *Lohengrin* to *Das Rheingold* is, the advance from that work to this Act is still more breathtaking, since the Act shows how Wagner can encompass a progression of emotions in a short space, leaving one with the impression, typical of him, that life has changed after this. The world is transformed by the advent of love: that sentimental cliché seems to achieve artistic dignity and strength through the glory of this Act, in which control and inspiration are in perfect balance. For the incestuous twins, of course, life can never be the same again: but for how much longer can it be better?

We, the audience, acquire a sense of that all too soon after the curtain rises on Act II. The Prelude, one of Wagner's most exciting, combines elements of the Wälsungs, with themes developed from the sword-motif and their love, an urgency suggestive of flight, and then, to enormously heavy scoring, the emergence for the first time of the Walküre motif. It is our first encounter with Wotan's favourite daughter, Brünn-hilde (her mother is Erda), in manic spirits at the thought of an impending battle at which she will do 'War Father's' (Wotan's) bidding. But she soon takes her leave, as she sees Fricka approaching – the battles *she* likes are not to Brünn-hilde's taste. And in a few moments we are back in the world of *Das Rheingold*, or that is how it seems at first. But before the strenuous argument between Fricka and Wotan has been under way for long, we realise that he is now a gentler, more troubled god, no longer even under the illusion that he is still on the ascendant, but rather fighting one of a series of rearguard actions. From this encounter, which becomes more painful for him and for us by the minute, he emerges humili-ated. His idea had been that the rule of law should be replaced by that of love, and Siegmund and Sieglinde were to be his prize specimens. But Fricka, arguing with the same cogency as Fasolt and Alberich in *Das Rheingold*, points out that if he abjures the rule of law, then no one need obey him; what he wants is to make the law up as he goes along, while she is the guardian of sacred, and thus eternal, laws of marriage. To his reply that the twins had followed their own law, that of their hearts, and that he had not been involved, Fricka reacts with shrewd, unanswerable contempt. Who created them? And how can a creator disclaim responsibility for what his creatures do?

Clearly we are back with one of Wagner's lifelong preoccupations: that of the 'absolute artist', alias a god who wants to share in the qualities of being fully human. In *Das Rheingold* we had the odd phenomenon of a god who tried to be, simultaneously, above the law and its exemplar, and made a miserable job of each. Here we have a god who claims to yield to the desires of his creations, but thereby offends against, indeed denies, the principles of his own wife, which are principles that he has delegated to her. With horrible accuracy Wagner shows us how Fricka is bound to win, since she is uninvolved with any of the characters she is arguing about. For her they are merely the prototypes of the wronged husband, the incestuous and adulterous twins, Wotan's illegitimate progeny. Wotan has become, as he certainly had not at any stage in *Das Rheingold*, someone who cares passionately about the existence and happiness of mortals for whom he feels the tenderness of a parent. It is not surprising that he appeals to what is new, since all this is new to him, and is affecting him more than anything that is old does. He had, as he explains later to Brünnhilde, begotten Siegmund and Sieglinde in order to do for him what he was unable to do for himself – to right the wrongs which he had done, but without knowledge of what they were doing. But quite apart from the issue of whether he could do that, he finds himself desperately concerned for their welfare.

Wotan has come, in short, to realise the necessity of new ways of feeling, which entails new people to have them. Few are as willing or able as he is to experience life freshly. Certainly Fricka is not, and is armed with reasons why she shouldn't be. Wagner gives marvellous expression to that in her exit number: after she has extracted from Wotan the oath that the Wälsung Siegmund shall fall in the forthcoming fight, she sings an arioso worthy of a baroque opera, and expressive of the kind of sentiments one finds there – 'Deiner ew'gen Gattin heilige Ehre beschirme heut' ihr Schild!' (Your eternal consort's holy honour her shield shall defend today!) – and she pauses briefly, the embodiment of self-confidence and self-righteousness, to speak to Brünnhilde.

The scene that follows is the moral and psychological heart of the drama, and of the whole cycle. Wotan is experiencing for the first time the complete thwarting of his plans, and is unable to do anything other than slump in misery, and then to cry out in his agony, to the same music and almost the same words as Alberich when Wotan had torn the Ring from his finger. Both realise the fathomlessness of their bondage. Alberich sings, 'Der Traurigen traurigster Knecht!' (The saddest of all sad slaves!), Wotan, 'Der Traurigste bin ich von Allen!' (I am the saddest of all beings!); Alberich had been caught by Wotan. Now Wotan is in an even worse position: 'In eig'ner Fessel fing ich mich' (I am caught in my own fetters). It is only Brünnhilde's capacity to identify with him, or to try to understand how he can be suffering as he is, that leads him into the long, excruciated monologue of self-searching in which he reconstructs the past to see how it could have become so intolerable a present, one from which he can see no future except 'Das Ende! Das Ende!' He tells Brünnhilde a good deal that we already know, more that we don't. From what we do know, it is clear that Wotan is being scrupulously accurate, at whatever cost to his self-esteem (and incidentally to the dismay of contemporary critics eager to find that he is an exemplification of that old-new concept, the unreliable narrator).

Everything leads to the point of no escape: 'der durch Verträge ich Herr, den Verträgen bin ich nun Knecht' (I who am lord through treaties am now the slave of treaties). And Wotan immediately moves on to his great hope, that a hero entirely ignorant of him should do what he can't do. But he at least half understands that that is not possible: 'Zum Ekel find' ich ewig nur mich in Allem was ich erwirke!' (To my disgust I find always only myself in whatever I effect!). In his extremity of bitterness he blesses Alberich's son, yet to be born, but clearly not a love-child; and hopes that he will destroy 'der Gottheit nichtigen Glanz' (the empty glitter of godhood). With that he has plumbed the depths of his self-loathing, and proceeds to give Brünnhilde her marching orders: Siegmund shall fall, Hunding shall vindicate marriage.

This scene is on a level of exploratory seriousness which is wholly new to opera, partly thanks to the number of factors which are involved, partly because Wagner uses his ever-developing powers to portray someone who has to recognise that the fundamental issues with which he is confronted are all within himself, and that the pressures he has been trying to avoid from the antagonists he has confronted cannot be vanquished by actions for which he has no responsibility – if there are any. This is not to say, as has been claimed, that the *Ring* is the anatomy of a single psyche: to see the other characters as projections of elements in Wotan is to effect a disastrous simplification and, in the end, de-dramatisation of the work. Though the monologue is obviously the most discursive part of the *Ring*, we do have to feel as well as think, and the carefully placed musico-dramatic climaxes ensure that we do.

Wotan begins, according to the directions, 'in a stifled, muffled voice', scarcely singing at all. He merely recounts, for some minutes, the point in his life where he lost the pleasure of youthful love (whatever that may have been) and began to yearn for power, and how that led to his deviousness. Attempting to be honest at a level which he has never, it seems, tried before, he proceeds along the time-honoured route that one takes in ultimate crises, that of trying to stick to 'the facts', uncoloured by feeling. But these facts precisely are about the progression of his feelings, and gradually his voice is coloured by self-reproach, bitterness, and glumly recalled moments of seeming success. The contrast with the world-destroying rage of a few minutes before is so striking that we stop contemplating his anguish, and find ourselves in a state, like Brünnhilde, of identification with him. The absence of any kind of posturing, the lack of self-exculpation or anything other than a candour that almost defies articulation, makes these bald opening stretches of Wotan's monologue one of Wagner's masterpieces of anti-rhetorical rhetoric. A highly dubious character, about whom we have had conflicting feelings, becomes at a stroke someone we cease to judge, instead joining him in trying to understand how he can have contrived so comprehensive a disaster for himself and everyone for whom he cares. So the fact that he is conveying a lot of information, which requires that we should be able to follow every word, since it is so complex, fits perfectly with the withdrawal of orchestral support.

As Wotan moves into territory with which we are familiar, *leitmotifs* from *Das Rheingold* creep into the orchestral texture, taking us back to what we had witnessed, but now rehearing it from the perspective of the chief protagonist in the drama. As he continues, revealing to Brünnhilde the stratagems he had employed for shoring up his morally undermined power, Wotan alternates between the hopes which he had and the ruin of those hopes that he faces, and is led ineluctably by the logic that Fricka had presented him with to his conclusion about his slave-like status. He reaches an insight which is familiar to Wagner's characters throughout his works: if he can't escape from his own limitations, then action of any kind is futile. In his other dramas, such tormented figures turn to a separate being, but in Wotan's restricted godhood there can be no truly separate being, since he will always have had a hand in their existence. 'Das And're, das ich ersehne, das And're erseh' ich nie; denn selbst muss der Freie sich schaffen' (The other for whom I long, the other I never see; for the free one must create himself). But if Wotan can give any sense to someone creating himself, it is only in terms of his being disobedient, or wholly ignorant, at least, of Wotan's designs, so that there is no guarantee that he will achieve the god's plans: on the contrary. This time round, the piling on of the agony by the orchestra is entirely inward – it voices Wotan's state. If one doesn't see that, then Wotan appears as no more than a guileful politician trapped by his own policies, which is how he is now almost always presented. That is to traduce one of the most shattering tragic effects any artist has contrived. At every level of his complex being Wotan is torn apart, and failure to grasp the horror of his plight, or attempts to reduce its dimensions, deprive us of insights into recurrent human agonies which are hardly to be gained elsewhere.

Having made us feel the full weight of Wotan's predicament, how does Wagner free us from the sense that a radically new moral vision – which is self-evidently necessary for us as much as for the inhabitants of the world of the *Ring* – is bound to be trapped in its own dialectic? By the most audacious of means: the experience of his art will bring about our freedom. How could that be? Only if the art itself possessed such transcendent authority that it was able, at one blow, to sweep away the accumulated traditions by which we live, or by which, as it is now customary to say, we are 'constituted', and replace our old feelings with a set of new ones which are self-evidently superior. This is the implicit imperative in all of Wagner's mature works. They don't issue the command that emerges from Rilke's Archaic Torso of Apollo, 'Du musst dein Leben ändern' (You must change your life). They do change it – or that is the idea. But that seems to take us back yet again to the 'absolute artist', an idea of which Wagner was suspicious. There is no question that those who feel most dubious about his art feel that he is making a devilish bid for their souls, just as those who are most spellbound by it are happy to give themselves into its, or his, keeping. But that is a matter to be postponed until the very end, since it is evidently the ultimate issue.

Meanwhile, back to the Second Act of *Die Walküre*. Wotan 'storms away', leaving a dejected Brünnhilde to collect her now heavy weapons for the fight. As she leaves the scene, the Wälsungs come onto it, Sieglinde distraught, Siegmund vainly trying to calm her. She is overcome with self-disgust that she had ever yielded to Hunding, wholly inconsolable. And she is terrified that in the forthcoming combat Hunding will slaughter Siegmund. Finally she faints, Siegmund rests her head in his lap, and the stage is set for the turning-point of the whole cycle, the so-called 'Annunciation of Death'.

Brünnhilde appears and gravely commands Siegmund to look at her. There follows a series of questions from Siegmund, answers from Brünnhilde, as to what she is, where she will take him, whom he will see in Valhalla. When Siegmund learns that Sieglinde must remain on earth, he declares his intention of staying with her. He has no interest in 'Walhall's spröden Wonnen' (Valhalla's paltry splendours) if he is to be separated from the one being he cares about. Brünnhilde is amazed. 'Does this poor woman, exhausted and sorrowful, mean everything to you?' she asks incredulously. Slowly, as Siegmund becomes ever more truculent, it begins to dawn on Brünnhilde what human love involves. And when Siegmund threatens to draw his sword and kill his sister-bride and himself, she is overcome by this manifestation of a kind of relationship of which she has had no inkling before. The scene has built up with majestic solemnity and grandeur, pathos and bemusement. And it gathers a momentum which leads to Brünnhilde's decision with inexorable, exhilarating abandon: she will disobey Wotan's command, defend Siegmund in battle and . . .

That is not, of course, what happens, or rather only some of it does. Wotan appears just as Siegmund, protected by Brünnhilde, is about to strike Hunding dead. Siegmund's sword, planted in the tree for him by Wotan, is shattered on Wotan's spear, and Hunding kills him. Wotan has upheld the laws of marriage, kept his word to Fricka, and the result is felt as cosmic catastrophe. Love has been defeated, Wotan's for his children and theirs for one another; and the compassion which their plight awakened in Brünnhilde, making her into a different person from the whooping warrior maid, means that she will be the object of Wotan's vengeance. Wotan gazes in anguish at his son's body, momentarily paralysed with grief. Then he dismisses Hunding to Fricka's presence in a hoarse whisper, and sets off in pursuit of Brünnhilde, who has gathered up the fragments of the sword and departed with Sieglinde.

Wagner could not, more economically and with surer

dramaturgic skill, have written an act in which we are put into a more frightful state. The First Act seemed to inaugurate a new world. The Second revokes it with such devastating logic that it seems as if there is no further possibility open to us. Wotan has by this point reached tragic stature, but unlike most tragic figures who are driven to unspeakable deeds, he has the prospect of continuing to live with what he has done for an eternity. And Brünnhilde is going to have to pay for her disobedience. It is this last issue which provides the content for Act III, though before Wotan arrives on the scene Brünnhilde has sent Sieglinde off into the forest, with the assurance that she is pregnant with the world's greatest hero. Then Brünnhilde awaits Wotan's decree, and most of the Act is occupied by the second huge scene between them, Brünnhilde telling Wotan that she only did what he truly wanted her to, Wotan condemning her for precisely that, since what he wants by this time is bound to be forbidden. Heartbroken but adamant, he realises that he must abandon his other adored child, or he will once more be guilty himself of not enforcing the laws by which he governs. The argument continues between them, until Wotan agrees that Brünnhilde will only be awoken from the sleep into which he is going to put her by the mightiest of heroes. But she will still lose her status as a goddess, that by which she is defined, so he leaves it wholly unclear as to what will eventually happen to her. But at this stage our concerns are more with what will happen to him, a god who has gained our sympathy at every point as he has become less godlike. The world without love seemed to be intolerably glacial; with love, it has become a scene of sheer suffering.

10

The Fearless Hero

It is easy to understand why *Die Walküre* is everyone's favourite *Ring* drama, at any rate so far as affection, rather than awe, is concerned. It is the only part of the cycle which is regularly performed alone, though it leaves things very much in the air. It is also not hard to see why *Siegfried* tends to be the least popular member of the cycle. Without the complex dialectics of *Das Rheingold* or the suffusing warmth and pain of *Die Walküre*, it presents a full-length study of a youthful hero whose main acts are to forge a sword, kill a dragon, then a dwarf, shatter Wotan's spear, and finally walk through a wall of fire to awaken an ex-goddess. This is the stuff of which fairy-tales are made, not parts of mythological epics.

The odd quality of *Siegfried*, which makes it more unlike Wagner's other works than they are unlike one another, comes from its strange origins; without a grasp of the position Wagner was in artistically when he wrote the text, and the still more bizarre facts of its musical composition, one is likely to approach it in the wrong way. That by itself will constitute an objection for those in the grip of critical dogmas about the independence of works of art from their genesis and their creator's intentions. Those who aren't will be able to rejoice in its unique properties.

A brief recapitulation of some crucial facts: Wagner's first idea was to write a single drama, *Siegfrieds Tod* (Siegfried's Death), but he was dissatisfied with the proportions of action

– Siegfried is, after all, meant to be a man of action – and explanation. One would have to take too much on trust, including the heroic deeds which Siegfried had performed and which would make his death a tragedy. So he moved backwards, composing a previous drama, *Der junge Siegfried* (Young Siegfried) in which the hero would be seen doing what otherwise would only be told. But he would, Wagner realised, have to be a character in a much earlier stage of development than the mature hero of *Siegfrieds Tod*, and the idiom in which he was portrayed would have to be correspondingly different. Writing to his intimate Theodor Uhlig in May 1851, he says, 'Have I not already written to you about a non-serious subject? It was about the lad who leaves home "to learn fear" and who is so stupid that he never learns what it is. Imagine my shock when I suddenly discovered that the lad in question is none other than – young Siegfried who wins the hoard and awakens Brünnhilde! – The matter is now resolved . . . "Young Siegfried" has the enormous advantage of conveying the important myth to an audience by means of actions on stage, just as children are taught fairy-tales. It will all imprint itself graphically by means of sharply defined physical images . . . Both works, however, will form totally independent pieces, which only on their first airing will be presented to the public in this particular order.'

Almost every sentence here is surprising. Above all one is astonished by the seemingly chancy way in which the *Ring*, at least in its last two parts, conceived first, came to contain what we now think of as its salient feature. And it is also striking how much Wagner was concerned to cater to popular tastes, make things easy for his audiences – an idea that he soon came to abandon with a vengeance. Wagner was constantly being surprised by 'finding' that separate characters in his works were 'in fact' the same, as if the world of his imagination were a pre-existent one which he was exploring: it seems that that is how it presented itself to him. The biggest omission from anything he writes at this stage, though, is any mention of Wotan and the gods. It seems that it was only as he came to see the radical nature of what he was doing that he needed to connect the story of Siegfried with another one which would creatively collide with it at all crucial junctures. In his original enthusiasm for 'the man of the future', whom he conceived Siegfried to be, he took it that we knew all about the man of the present, whom Wotan represents in quintessential form. But when he came to write the two previous parts of the cycle, his fascination with the psychology of the being who wants to move away from law into 'freedom' or 'love', but is unable to do so without disastrous consequences, took over to a point where, if asked offhand who was the *Ring*'s central figure, most people would probably say Wotan.

But the placing of Wotan as a, or the, central character of what now became the first two parts of the *Ring* meant that, if it was to achieve a true unity, Wotan couldn't be forgotten after the close of *Die Walküre*. By this stage he has acquired such tragic momentum that introducing him into *Siegfried*, as *Der junge Siegfried* rapidly became, was a big risk: how could this 'heroic comedy', as Wagner calls it in his autobiography, *Mein Leben*, or even 'heroic *opéra-comique*', his designation of it in a letter to Hans Richter, its first conductor, not be unbalanced by the presence – it could hardly be an incidental one – of someone who has all the heaviness that the happy young hero is blissfully unaware of?

The answer was that it couldn't, and that therefore, in line with Wagner's artistic temperament, if not the one he displayed often in life, *Siegfried* is a much more serious work, and one far fuller of anguished characters, than Wagner originally intended. But even if he had not felt constrained to bring

Wotan into the action, Wagner would have had to give Sieg-fried something to be heroic about. His quest to learn fear must involve him in confronting obstacles which the rest of us would find alarming. And although fairly strong elements of fairy-tale remain, once more Wagner has to give an identity to a character which enables us to recognise him from one drama to the next. So Mime, originally conceived in a benign form, becomes insidiously evil. Fafner, the giant turned dragon, is properly terrifying, even if Wagner can't resist giving him a sympathetic side. And Wotan, who in the first draft lets Siegfried pass on his way to the mountain-top, now once more interposes his spear against the sword Nothung, but this time with the opposite result from Act II of *Die Walküre*.

Hence the characters that surround Siegfried are all old acquaintances of ours, and of one another. What of the figure whom they frame, and whose story this essentially is? For the time being, at least, he has to be the sole representative of the new order, making the representatives of the old order look like the superannuated specimens they are. Wagner had clearly set himself an immense task. Love, in its recognisable, purely human form, had proved defenceless against the accumulated strength of tradition. But as we have every reason to know, tradition, however bankrupt, is unstoppable without violence and calculated irreverence expressed in brutal terms. So Siegfried, to overthrow it, has to be either very cunning or very strong. If very cunning, he is too likely to get involved in the same kind of plotting which characterises his opponents. If very strong, and prepared to use his strength, he is liable to forfeit our sympathies, since we are members of the old order too, at best in favour of judicious acts of reform, undertaken within the context of law.

Wagner had no choice: there is no indication that he wanted

any. He was sufficiently enamoured of his 'stupid' hero to paint him in unflinching primary colours, once more trusting in his power to transform our consciousness, so that we would see what had to happen, and gladly acquiesce in it. This was his major miscalculation, that audiences would find the young Siegfried sympathetic. On the contrary, he is routinely described as a young storm-trooper, a monster of ingratitude (Schopenhauer's reaction), an overgrown boy-scout (Ernest Newman, usually among the most sympathetic of commentators). It is easy to refute those charges, but a problem will still remain.

As to Siegfried's behaviour towards Mime, often taken to be the most objectionable element in his portrayal: it would be interesting to see how the people who recriminate with him over this would behave towards a whining little creature (smallness isn't necessarily charming) who spent half his time complaining about their ingratitude, was unwilling to answer their questions as to where they came from, and was furthermore the only company available to them. Siegfried's preference for the beasts of the forest strikes me as fully understandable. And guileless as he is, he has enough sense to feel suspicious of Mime's motives in looking after him. In any case, the action of the drama fully exculpates Siegfried, since we learn that, however ludicrously, Mime is as intent on world domination as Alberich, and in pursuit of that end attempts to poison Siegfried after he has slain Fafner.

The trouble seems to be not, as is usually alleged, that Wagner draws Mime too unsympathetically, but rather the reverse. He conveys to us what misery it is to be Mime, and thus tends to elicit our protectiveness. Whereas what, throughout his work, Wagner was intent on communicating is the way in which wretchedness makes vile. 'Hate the happy!' Alberich memorably enjoins his son Hagen in the shattering opening scene of Act II of *Götterdämmerung*, but he has no need, because it is so clear that he does (and he has already said so). Misery is both hateful and hate-begetting, and that is the final truth about Mime. But why a dwarf? In large part the answer is provided by the fairy-tale elements in the plot, in which the inner qualities of characters are manifest in what they look like – one doesn't go to these sources for political correctness. As for Siegfried's treatment of the other figures who stand in his way, or threaten him, it would be merely tiresome to offer vindications, when anyone who wants them is evidently too obtuse to benefit from them.

What, it seems to me, can more plausibly be alleged against Siegfried is not his negative characteristics, but his comparative lack of positive ones. He is fearless, which means (I think, but I am not confident about my grasp of the concept of courage) that he is not brave: he has nothing to overcome in himself. Fear is, moreover, something he has to learn, but this element in the plot tends to become recessive. He has an affinity for nature, and in his self-communings by the brook in Act II, usually known as 'Forest Murmurs', he gives generous, moving expression to them. The music here is identical in substance to that in *Das Rheingold* when Loge describes the omnipresence of love, but the difference in effect is extraordinary – the gap between the inveterate ironist and someone who could never know what irony was. Siegfried wants congenial company, even hoping that Fafner might provide it, and if possible a mate, taking the creatures he has observed in the forest as role-models. But there is scant indication that he has much in the way of a sex-drive. He is strong, but we affect not to find that an admirable quality, though it is possible that it might come back into fashion, and of course in some circles – not, on the whole, Wagner-listening ones – already has done. How stupid is he? Conventional views have it that he is very stupid, but I find it hard to see why. What things should he do that he doesn't? Or not do that he does?

In the end it comes down to the question of whether Siegfried is sufficiently interesting to deserve a whole long drama virtually to himself, when we have the far more intriguing and involving figure of Wotan spending most of his time in the wings, and appearing, lightly disguised, only as the Wanderer. But to that Wagner, at any rate, would answer that it begs the central question. We, like Wotan, as men of the present, are bound to be more interested in him than in an unspoiled child of nature, unless we make the effort, a vast one, to overcome our prized sophistication and rejoice in the company of a new-minted simplicity. But how new-minted is it? In terms of the *Ring*, Siegfried does mark a fresh start, but is it one which holds any promise – where can it lead? Whenever the Wanderer appears, with his ineffably noble accompaniment, a god now resigned to his supersession, who comes, he says, 'zu schauen, nicht zu schaffen' (to observe, not to act), his are the strains that go to our hearts. But the price of such genuine grandeur is an abdication from life, one more indication that Wotan grows more sympathetic the less he interferes in the world. Meanwhile, as Siegfried proceeds with his disposal of the unsavoury past, destroying no doubt in order to create, we eagerly wait to see what he will create. So far – by the end of Act II – he hasn't suffered enough for us to care much about him. That may say more about us than about him.

But Wagner felt the same way, it seems. One of the most celebrated episodes in the history of creation is his abandonment of his hero at the end of Act II, just as the Woodbird is teasingly leading him on the path to Brünnhilde, and thus to happiness. Wagner was at home with suffering: 'There is a musician who, more than any other musician, is a master at finding the tones in the realm of suffering, depressed, and tortured souls, at giving language even to mute misery. None can equal him in the colours of late autumn, in the indescribably moving happiness of the last, truly last, truly shortest joy ... as the Orpheus of all secret misery he is greater than any ... But he does not *want* to be that! His characters prefer large walls and audacious frescoes.' That, of course, is Nietzsche once more, in his final polemic against Wagner. And the truth in those words is confirmed by Wagner's audacious decision to leave the *Ring* on one side and return to it after he had written something that stood a better chance of immediate performance. The darkness of his mood, more reflected in than called into being by his continued perusal of Schopenhauer, and the torment of the greatest passion of his life, for Mathilde Wesendonck, counted at least as much in his unwillingness to take Siegfried up the mountain at that stage, and in his irresistible need to embark on 'the most simple, but full-blooded conception' of a work on the Tristan legend.

Finally, he must have realised that the problem he had posed for himself in the *Ring* was one which, for the moment, he was in no state to tackle. The *Ring* was intended to be, and did eventually become, his great commentary on human society and its possibilities. But there is a large gap between the fearless Siegfried who has never yet met another human being, and a work which takes to its conclusion the issues raised in *Das Rheingold* about social existence. For the time being he needed to explore the condition which is at the extreme from that: complete absorption of one person in another, to the exclusion of the world. Siegmund and Sieglinde had not only opened up this new horizon, to have it curtly, brutally cut off. They had also enabled Wagner to compose with a lyrical freedom which none of the rest of the *Ring* would allow him. He had to find the answer to the question, always more urgent than any other in his own life: was such love as the Wälsungs knew doomed only by its conflict with society, or did its own logic lead to death?

11

The Passion of Passion

It is widely known that Wagner wrote a religious drama, but not so widely realised which of his works that is. *Tristan und Isolde*, often described as a paean to sensuality, a hymn to romantic love, even an exposé of its impossibility, is the work in question. It is the one work of Wagner's which seems to be making an unconditional demand on our capacity to embrace a new, redeeming doctrine. Along with Bach's St Matthew Passion, it is one of the two greatest religious works of our culture. Bach had the easier task, for he was writing in the midst of a culture which accepted the religion to which he gave unsurpassable expression. There was a long tradition of passions, many of them of a very high quality, which he had to draw on. His achievement lay in producing a work which, if it does not eclipse the others, renders them in the last resort unnecessary as a statement of the Christian's ultimate article of faith.

By contrast, Wagner had to define the religion to which he gave expression. Not only that, but the definition had to be couched in terms precise enough to distinguish this faith from many apparently similar ones which have been going the rounds for a very long time. History, and the history of the arts, is full of great lovers, usually doomed, and it is easy to think that Wagner did nothing more than produce an extreme case of tragic love. But the first thing to realise about *Tristan und Isolde* is that it is not a tragedy, or if it is, only one of a most peculiar kind. That immediately separates it from any major treatment we have of Dido and Aeneas, Antony and Cleopatra, Romeo and Juliet, Phaedra and Hippolytus, or any other famous pair who have received the full tragic treatment from consummate artists.

That is not to deny that *Tristan* is suffused with tragic feeling. But it is important to draw a distinction between that and a tragedy. If it were a tragedy, it couldn't be a religious work. The St Matthew Passion is also suffused with tragic feeling, but its redemptive ending, or hope, similarly precludes it from final tragic status. I make these bald statements without further expansion, because I hope what they denote about my attitude to tragedy will emerge as I consider the substance of *Tristan*.

The Prelude to *Tristan*, Wagner's most renowned contribution to the history of music, is something more than that. It is a contribution to the history of the Western mind, quite apart from music. It is so complete an expression of the yearning which permeates the whole work that one might, if one listened to it and no more (as many people are happy to do, and often), assume that it must pre-empt what follows in the same way that we saw the Prelude to *Lohengrin* doing. The miracle of *Tristan* is that the whole work lives up to the Prelude, even though the climax of that has been the object of vain emulation ever since it was composed – Wagner wisely never tried anything along those lines again. The point about the Prelude – all musicological points aside, and it has spawned books of them – is something that its imitators, such as Richard Strauss and Scriabin, have uniformly missed. Its climax manages both to clinch everything which precedes it and yet still to be a non-fulfilment. It is, that climax, yearning, not its consummation, taken to its ultimate point; and so we have to have the drama if we are not to feel mere exhaustion.

Since all the relevant 'action' of *Tristan* takes place in the orchestra, the singers only giving conceptual expression to it, and thereby making it intelligible at the same time as they make it bearable (an insight memorably expressed by Nietzsche, still a Wagnerian, in *The Birth of Tragedy*), it is appropriate that the drama proper should begin with an unaccompanied song – we know that it is not part of the content of the work – of poignant sadness, lamenting the Young Sailor's distance from his Irish maiden. But Isolde takes this, as she takes everything, to refer to her, and launches on to the first of what are to be many outbursts in Act I. Anything outside the world of Tristan and Isolde only registers as it affects them, in their state of exalted stalemate, for most of Act I; rhapsodic striving for a comprehension of their feelings in Act II; and desperate longing for union, with final isolated consummations, in Act III. Wagner stresses the irrelevance of the external world in each act by beginning with it, in order for it to be brusquely excluded. What the Sailor's Song does in Act I is performed by the distant hunting horns in Act II, and by the desolate Shepherd's piping in Act III. But increasingly, from act to act, the 'real' world of everyone else, and the illusory world to Tristan and Isolde, is incorporated into *their* real world, the world of passion.

In the centre of the work, at the climax of the most famous part of the so-called love duet, 'O sink' hernieder, Nacht der Liebe' (Oh sink upon us, night of love), the lovers sing together, 'selbst dann bin ich die Welt' (then I myself am the world), an astoundingly audacious claim, which means that they have expanded to embrace everything, or everything has contracted to satisfy their joint solipsism. One might have expected, given that they were going to be so extravagant, that they would say 'we' rather than 'I', and if they were only a little less extraordinary that is what they would have said. But

Wagner gives them the logic of their convictions: if each of them is the world, then they are one another. That, too, is something from which they don't flinch, as they move on to the final stretch of the duet, and do indeed exchange names, that is identities, building up on wave after wave of orchestral sound, in what is without competition as the longest, most extreme climax in music – and still they have not achieved what they were striving for, precisely because they are still in a state of striving.

This last section (which almost always fails to come off in performance, because it demands a controlled abandonment which virtually no one can manage to conduct or sing) is begun by Tristan, quite clearly intoning in erotic-liturgical mode, and then taken up by Isolde, as they alternate and then unite: 'So stürben wir um ungetrennt, ewig einig ohne End', ohn' Erwachen, ohn' Erbangen, namenlos in Lieb' umfangen, ganz uns selbst gegeben, der Liebe nur zu leben!' (So might we die together, eternally one without end, without awakening, without fearing, nameless in love's embrace, giving ourselves wholly, to live only for love!). This is the nearest they come to fulfilment together, for here they are calm, ecstatic. But after Brangäne has warned them that day will soon take over from night, they become frenzied, uttering things they don't understand, and it is almost a relief to us, if not to them, when they are caught in the act by King Marke and the hunters.

Time and again in *Tristan* one wonders whether things can go any further, and they do. Even in Act I, where Tristan and Isolde are still fully recognisable people, their extremes of intensity, almost all of it horribly pent-up, suggest imminent expiring, which is indeed what they hope for, and think they have within their grasp, once they have drunk the potion – the love-potion, thanks to Brangäne's well-intentioned meddling, while Isolde's command had been for the death potion.

(Regrettably, it is still necessary to stress that, so far as its long-term effects are concerned, they might as well have been drinking water. The potion enables them to release their previously hidden feelings for one another instantly, but they do that only because they believe that death is imminent.) They are, up to this point, a couple of identifiable-with characters, who are kept apart by resentment, pride, chivalry, misplaced sense of duty, justified sense of betrayal. Wagner never takes us into unknown regions until we have our bearings. And those are not decisively abandoned until we have had a scrupulously careful indictment of the limitations and illusions of 'the world of Day'. When the lovers have concluded their case against the Day, that is the world in which they have up to now foolishly dwelt, they are free to begin the exploration which takes them into regions no one has previously explored, except mystics seeking for a very different kind of union. This is humanism pressed to its limits, then exploded into transcendent metaphysics, in which the self ceases to suffer by becoming the other self, the other person, whose apartness is the cause of all the suffering. It is this which Wagner depicts in the closing minutes of the duet, and then, with analytic exactitude, in most of Act III.

In Act II, after the abrupt interruption of the duet, we have had the 'world's' case stated at its most moving and comprehensive in King Marke's tragic reproaches of Tristan. When he concludes by asking how such a betrayal could have occurred, we have, in Tristan's answer, an *approfondissement* which prepares us for the subsequent act, by far Wagner's greatest achievement to date. Tristan can't tell Marke what he needs to know; instead, he turns to Isolde, and to the accompaniment of the act's most ravishing music – a pity no one is listening by this stage – he asks her to follow him to the land where he came from, 'das Wunderreich der Nacht' (the wonder-realm of Night), which he left for this illusory world. Isolde is as gently insistent on following as he is on leaving, and they kiss. Melot the betrayer forces a fight, which Tristan is eager to lose. He drops his defence, and Melot wounds him, as the noble Marke tries to restrain him. It is Tristan's second attempt to die, but death refuses to be so easy a victor.

One of the advantages of the gramophone, or whatever it should now be called, is that it enables us to stop there and wait until we can cope with Act III; an advantage the tenor singing Tristan must be still more grateful for. What lies ahead is an artistic and spiritual challenge to our capacities for response such as no artist had dared to issue before. Wagner himself realised that he was now involved in a composition which had no exemplars. He was not boasting when he wrote to Mathilde Wesendonck, while he was in Lucerne writing this incredible music: 'Child! This Tristan is turning into something *terrible*! This final Act!!!!—I fear the opera will be banned – unless the whole thing is parodied in a bad performance –: only mediocre performances can save me! Perfectly *good* ones will be bound to drive people mad,– I cannot imagine it otherwise.'

It is at this stage that we realise that the opera is much more about Tristan than it is about Isolde – or rather about the Tristan who has achieved his metaphysical insight in Act II, and is thus remotely related to the paragon of chivalry of Act I. The symmetries of *Tristan*, which make it so compelling a drama even at the ordinary level, are up to a point misleading. Act I concentrates on Isolde, but the outraged Irish princess who is prepared for death (in the everyday sense) rather than marriage to 'Kornwalls müden König' (Cornwall's weary King). This Isolde is tormentedly in love with Tristan, but not in a way to create any metaphysical ripples. Act I is a stupendous psychological drama, worked out with remarkable economy and thoroughness, but all directed to showing the comparatively superficial level of merely human passion. One only realises that later – in the first encounters one has with *Tristan*, it is Act I which creates the strongest effect.

In Act II, from Isolde's sublime invocation of Frau Minne (the goddess of a previously unheard-of love) onwards, psychology is rendered pointless for the rest of the act, so far as the lovers are concerned. It is a demolition of the very notion which psychology presupposes, that of the self in relation to other selves and the external world. That is why it is absurd to complain, or even merely to observe, that Tristan and Isolde are very much wrapped up in their own feelings, or that they are exploiting one another's states of mind, or that Wagner is revealing how essentially egoistic romantic love makes people, or – the most crass criticism of all, but one which is still often heard – that Tristan and Isolde are incorrigibly garrulous, when they should be acting rather than talking: 'Oh, get your leg over and stop going *on* about it,' as the *Times* critic I quoted in Chapter 2 succinctly put the point. One of the functions of Marke's great monologue is to take us back, with gentle sympathy, to the level at which people try to understand motives, to react to betrayal, as they see it, and to look for the possibility of forgiving what seems unforgivable. When Tristan, in reply to Marke's first expressions of shock, 'with convulsive violence' ejaculates, 'Tagsgespenster! Morgenträume! täuschend und wüst! Entschwebt! Entweicht!' (Phantoms of day! Morning dreams! deceiving and void! Vanish! Away!) we are as appalled as Marke, until we recall that Tristan has moved into a world where what he is hearing is just nonsense.

Wagner, scrupulously fair to unbelievers, as one would hardly expect an evangelist to be, gives Marke the opportunity to spell out at length the set of terms which the work has for the previous forty-five minutes been undermining. This is the 'absolute artist' introducing a note of doubt, warning us that if we don't side with Marke we are in for a journey which Tristan gives the most restrained indications of, but which we already know from the near-insanities of the duet will demand 'not less than everything'. He, Tristan, regains his chivalrous attitude once he has composed himself. The peremptoriness of Christ in telling the rich young man that unless he instantly abandons everything he values and follows him, he has no hope, is not Tristan's way, because he realises that 'the world of Day' is one in which most people will always live, and that only a tiny elect can even understand what he is saying. Tristan is in this respect an 'elitist' because he is a realist.

The 'world of Day' is given a further, if indirect, boost by the Prelude to Act III: late Romanticism begins here. It is oppressive, sultry, claustrophobic, constantly on the verge of extinction from its own heavy burden. And nothing is done to lighten the mood by the huge, weird, relentlessly unending melody that the Shepherd is playing as the curtain rises. Tristan is now alone, and the only impression the outside world makes on him is this melody which strikes us as coming from another time and place, but which, in due course, will come to symbolise for Tristan all the misery that has made up his life. What, we might wonder, is to be gained by so unflinching a contact with truths which the human spirit can only be obliterated by? But we will wonder in vain, because it is not as if Tristan had any choice in the matter. He is, as Isolde has presciently remarked early in Act I, a 'Tod-geweihtes Herz' (death-consecrated heart). And he spends the Third Act living out his destiny with an honesty which only the delirium of final illness could induce, or permit.

Once more Wagner lowers us, as it were, gradually into

the state which he is going to hold us in. The Shepherd is uncomprehending of Tristan's condition as anything other than that of a man who has received a severe sword wound. Kurwenal, now a moving figure with inklings, necessarily faint, of the nature of Tristan's distress, tells the Shepherd that he wouldn't understand, something that Tristan will soon be telling Kurwenal. When Tristan finally emerges into consciousness, Kurwenal's joy is unbounded, but it is all the more affecting because it is beside the point. Tristan has been 'im weiten Reich der Weltennacht' (in the wide realm of the world's Night), experiencing 'göttlich ew'ges Urvergessen' (divine, eternal primal forgetfulness), so as soon as he sees the light – almost the whole of Act III cruelly takes place in the blinding, baking sun – he is once more put on the rack of 'Sehnsucht' (yearning), the keyword of this act and of the whole drama. The music rises quickly to a pitch of intolerable intensity as Tristan realises that Isolde is still in the realm of the sunlight, that he was alone in the realm of Night. He longs, as he had when he was waiting for her to extinguish the torch in Act II, for the light to die, instead of forever awakening his pain. This is the first of his great cycles of agony, carried to lengths which might well have induced Wagner to write to Mathilde as he did, were it not that the second cycle will be far worse.

There follows the scene in which Tristan, told by Kurwenal that he has sent for Isolde, hallucinates her arrival, screaming in ecstasy at the approach of the non-existent ship, until the Shepherd's original melody cuts all that off, and he knows that he is to continue to endure what would kill him if it were not the only thing that is keeping him alive – his longing. Throughout the frightful scene that follows, the Shepherd's tune winds as the bringer of all the terrible tidings that Tristan has ever received. Every significant experience of his life is recalled, all brought to focus in the drinking of the potion, now the symbol of his torment. As climax follows unimaginable climax, he realises that he himself brewed the potion, that all the pain he suffers comes from within, from his being at all, and the realisation all but kills him, so that he ends cursing the potion and him (Tristan himself) who made it; and collapses unconscious.

Kurwenal, as distraught, on his own level, as his master, cries out, 'O Minnetrug! O Liebeszwang! Der Welt holdester Wahn!' (Oh deception of love! Oh passion's force! The most beautiful of the world's illusions!), and thereby gives food for thought. Is he only voicing his own horror at the state Tristan has been reduced to, or is he, like a traditional Fool, wiser than the hero? The perspective from which he speaks wouldn't permit him to think anything different, but what is the perspective of the whole work, or does it have more than one? It is hard to know whether these questions should even be raised, if they can't be answered. We live in a critical climate in which it is seen as crucial to pounce on moments of what are almost inadvertence, and take them as functioning in a way comparable to Freudian slips, the more significant because of their incongruity with the main thrust of the work at hand. Wagner offers many opportunities for practising this kind of criticism, at the same time as his art seems by its nature to want to resist it. With *Tristan*, so paralysingly absolute in its demands, we are given a motive for letting ourselves off its piercing hook, but the work seems to have sunk itself too deeply into us.

Tristan, meanwhile, returns yet again to consciousness, but this time, having purged himself with the savagery of his curse, his mood is one of ecstatic calm, and after tentative further enquiries about the ship he produces his own vision, to which reality is irrelevant, of Isolde crossing the sea as if over fields of flowers, smiling at him in consolation, bringing him release.

He ends, with vast, serene orchestral waves supporting him, 'Ach, Isolde, Isolde, wie schön bist du!' (Ah, Isolde, Isolde, how beautiful you are!). Essentially he has found the world that he wants to be in, but there is still this world to be coped with – the actual arrival of the ship this time, his madly tearing his bandages off, his 'hearing' the light being extinguished, and his staggering across the stage, dying, as Isolde arrives. That action is all very thrilling, but Tristan's pilgrimage was already complete. He had his moment of highest exaltation, alone.

Now it is Isolde who is alone, and alive. She responds with incredulity to this new and, as she sees it, still more terrible betrayal by Tristan. They had vowed to die together, and those are the only terms on which she will accept death. She pours out her anguish over Tristan, but when its climax has passed she thinks she sees him wake, and sinks unconscious over him. But the world intrudes one last time, as the slaves of illusion troop on, fight, kill one another, repent, lament, do the things that people do. Marke tries to make Isolde understand, but in gaining her new set of concepts she has lost her grip on the old. She is ready for the recapitulation of the final passage of the Act II duet, but with its striving, which had seemed to be its essence, transcended and made into a floating motion (Wagner, not usually susceptible to the visual arts, always found Titian's *Assumption of the Virgin* in the Frari uniquely inspiring). Isolde, convinced that Tristan is smiling at her, ascends, or is submerged, with him to a point where she can be absorbed 'in des Welt-Atems wehendem All' (in the world-breath's encompassing all), and her final words, as she sinks 'as if transfigured', Wagner carefully writes, are 'unbewusst, höch'ste Lust!' (unconscious, highest bliss!).

'To this day I am still looking for a work that equals the dangerous fascination and the shuddering and sweet infinity of *Tristan* – and look in all the arts in vain. All the strangenesses of Leonardo da Vinci emerge from their spell at the first note of *Tristan*. This work is emphatically Wagner's *non plus ultra* ... The world is poor for anyone who has never been sick enough for this "voluptuousness of hell": it is permitted, it is almost imperative, to employ a formula of the mystics at this point.' Nietzsche again, this time in his autobiography *Ecce Homo*, explaining how Wagner was a benefactor to him in that he enabled him to rise to this supreme challenge to his health.

One sees what he means. It seems that either one must in some way embrace *Tristan*, or else regard it as a work which is so dangerous as to be dignified, at best, as the eternal example of the harm a work of art can do. Or even, as I suggested at the beginning of the chapter, recategorise it as a religious work, only called 'art' because of the promiscuous capaciousness of that term now. But if *Tristan* does announce a new religion, it seems that all its adherents have been heretics, since no one actually puts it into practice, because it is unclear how one would set about doing that. It is not so much that it is unintelligible; probably all religions are, certainly Christianity, with its central doctrine of three persons who are the same person, a sublime paradox or arrant contradiction, according to taste, which nothing in *Tristan* trumps. But Christianity promises everything in a timeless future, while *Tristan* seems to demand action now, and even paradise immediately thereafter. One sees why downright commentators seize on Isolde's final words and say that if you are unconscious it is hard to be in a state of highest bliss.

And Kurwenal's denunciation of love as the most beautiful of illusions has its appeal too. For, as I have already indicated, both Tristan and Isolde reach their most elevated state of mind in isolation, visionaries who create the object of their ecstasy. They have spent a great part of the opera denouncing the world and its daylight illusions, only, it seems, to fall prey to their own night-begotten fantasies. And anyway, why should we believe any of what they sing, just because it is set to music which has a compelling beauty of a kind that none other possesses? The only answer to that question is that the experience of love at its most intense becomes an intuition that its fulfilment can only be found in a renunciation of the self, undertaken all the more willingly because the tortures of being a self are so intolerable. It is the seriousness with which Wagner expresses and explores that intuition that leads me to say that in the end *Tristan* is a religious work. It has, as religious works customarily do, the relentlessness and exclusiveness of eliminating alternatives, putting those characters other than the lovers in the position of non-comprehenders or betrayers. Even the devoted and adoring Brangäne and Kurwenal are abused by their mistress and master respectively for failure to grasp what is truly happening.

The trouble with accounts of *Tristan* which view it as in any way a critique or exposé of romantic love is that that is not in the least how it feels. A considerable time after one's last experience of the work one may well begin to think that Kurwenal is right, even if his moment of truth receives very little emphasis. But that certainly is not how one feels during or for some time after listening to it, as Nietzsche, the more impressive a witness because of his general hostility to Wagner, provides the most eloquent testimony to. The phenomenon of *Tristan-Rausch* (Tristan intoxication) is too widespread and continuing to be overlooked – there is a book on the subject, with an imposing list of those who have succumbed to the intoxication. Perhaps the most one can say – it seems very lame, but it is hard to imagine what wouldn't in the presence of this work – is that it takes what is, for many people, a covert doctrine, makes it tactlessly explicit, one of Wagner's specialities, and shows where it leads if taken with a seriousness which most people shy away from. It is hardly a critique of *Tristan* to say that most people who espouse a romantic view take it much less far. One might as well criticise Christ because of the Church of England. Every religion is of its essence a doctrine of extremes; many people love the thought of extremes, but not the practice. They are delighted that there are works in which the practice is demonstrated, but convert it into an aesthetic experience for easy digestion. That is what the St Matthew Passion enables them to do, though it cannot have been what Bach intended. It is less clear what Wagner intended. Before he composed *Tristan*, he wrote in a letter to Liszt that he wanted 'to erect a monument to this most beautiful of all dreams'. It might be that that is the last word, as well as the first, on *Tristan*. But there is still an enormous amount to say in between, most of it as yet unsaid, despite the vast 'literature' it has generated.

Wagner was taken aback by what he had written. He had hoped that he was going to produce something which was more practical for contemporary staging than the *Ring* would be. He soon realised that that was not what had eventuated. So, incorrigibly optimistic as this heterodox follower of Schopenhauer always remained, he tried once more to come up with something that the current opera houses and their audiences could easily cope with. But he must, as a most reflective artist, have had other motives, especially in the light of what he went on to create. His fear, only slightly exaggerated for comic effect, that good performances of *Tristan* would drive people mad, led him to a sustained meditation on the role and responsibility of the artist in relation to his society, a central concern of his next music drama. *Tristan* is not only about two characters who regard society with contempt, but it also turned out to be wholly indifferent to the effects it might have on its audiences. Should the artist remain true to his daimon, as Wagner so conspicuously had, and not give a damn for how it would alter people's consciousness? Or were there subtle questions to be dealt with, ones which might seem recalcitrant to artistic treatment, but if they received it successfully, reveal that the creator of *Tristan* knew that his daimon was, after all, not the only object of his responsibility?

I feel intensely dissatisfied with these remarks on *Tristan*, because however much one stresses its singularity, one still wants to understand: and to understand is in large part to assimilate something to other things. Drawing a circle round a work and saying what it isn't like is not enough; nor, in this particular instance, is making the comparison with the St Matthew Passion, not because that doesn't have some point, but because Bach's masterpiece, as the work which more than any other embodies the fundamental beliefs of our civilisation during its greatest period, achieves something which is, in the best sense, monumental, and a monument to something which, because it has been around so long, we feel at home with, even if we reject it. But *Tristan* is in key ways the opposite of that. It is a work of anti-civilisation, and its appeal, the violent and profound effect it has on us, is intimately bound up with that. Even if we don't subscribe to the gospel of passion which it promulgates, we may still be stirred to the depths by a perfect manifestation – and we judge perfection, however much we might resist doing so, in terms of tradition: what else? – of subversiveness. *Tristan* has all the classical virtues, put to the most drastically non-classical ends. Its formal impeccableness is solely devoted to propagating the values of something that lies below the level at which form can get a grasp.

Tristan, in other, and for the time being last, words, is an impossible achievement. We worship it partly because we are unable to understand it; that is another of its qualifications for religious status. Wagner judged to a T the degree to which, in order to found a new religion, it was necessary to make it incomprehensible. If we were to understand it, we could 'place' it in relation to other works, and love it without fear. Since we can't, we have to accept that it is there, eternally seductive and eternally elusive. Nietzsche was right to view it with superstitious awe. It marks, more than anything else, the defeat of criticism.

12

Art, Tradition and Authority

The contrasts between *Tristan* and *Die Meistersinger von Nürnberg*, which Wagner almost immediately went on to write, seem to be almost complete. Since Wagner generally starts as he means to go on, we might compare the openings of the two works. There is the painful whisper of *Tristan*, the tremulous beginnings of passion, leading to the so-called 'Tristan chord' which will keep analysts busy as long as their pursuit remains legal. And there is the gloriously confident stride of *Die Meistersinger*, beginning with a C major chord, the paradigm of Western tonal music. Where *Tristan*, if not quite mono-thematic (musically speaking), approaches that condition, at least for the music of its two central characters, *Die Meister-singer* shows a Haydnesque fertility of and delight in invention, much of it carelessly discarded as soon as it has been played once (David's recital of the Modes). Variety of characters, no single leading subject (I have even seen *Die Meistersinger* criticised for not being 'about' anything, which suggests that the critic could only respond to works that are about one thing). A firm allegiance to the values of the Day – the Second Act, which takes place at night, ends in a brutal riot, as nocturnal escapades are wont to do; and in his great 'Wahn' monologue in Act III, Hans Sachs dwells with pained bemusement on what went on at night, and then turns, as the music does too, with great relief, to greet Midsummer's Day, when there is as little darkness as possible. Instead of two death-devoted lovers achieving their delusive aim, two happy young things united in the prospect of marriage. Even, daringly, a passing quotation from *Tristan* to demonstrate that Sachs has no intention of playing King Marke. A committee-meeting set to flowing, glowing melodies which truly do transfigure the untransfigurable. And the climax of the work, the ineffable Quintet, which not only appears to break Wagner's self-denying ordinance against ensembles, but suggests a contentment with this world that would make any efforts to transcend it both supererogatory and absurd.

That is the standard image of *Die Meistersinger*, and I don't want to say that it is wrong. But it is damagingly incomplete, not only because it neglects the crueller aspects of the work, always to be expected when we encounter comedy, but because it so ignores the explicit philosophising that Sachs goes in for, and then – revealing him as a most atypical philosopher – proceeds to put into practice. This is, it must be said, a mischievous work, almost a musical crossword, in which Wagner constantly diverts our attention from what he is most interested in. The greatest and most fascinating contrast between *Tristan* and *Die Meistersinger* is not that one is preoccupied with metaphysics, and the other unconcerned with it, but that Wagner moves from his most patently doctrinal work to his most covertly instructive one.

The teasing begins in the magnificent Prelude, one of Wagner's most virtuoso displays of the traditional German skills of playing around with themes, combining them, parodying them, making them part of a grand procession which ends in overwhelming splendour. It proclaims itself as the specimen *in excelsis* of the overture as potpourri, with what we will come to recognise as the music of the Mastersingers themselves, their apprentices, the ardour of the young lovers, the Prize Song with which Walther von Stolzing will win Eva's hand, the mockery of the crowd when Beckmesser, the comic villain, attempts to sing the Prize Song himself. It seems as if we have all the elements here of a rich comic drama, the framework established in terms of which things will be worked out. But oddly, and puzzlingly, that is not the case. For there is no hint, in the Prelude, of the central figure of Sachs. Not, of course, that one demands, even in so rich a potpourri, that all the ingredients should be presented. But as *Die Meistersinger* progresses, it turns so much into Sachs's work that we must be surprised that he receives no mention in so powerfully mood-setting a piece.

In fact, it is a consummate stroke of Wagner's to exclude him. For it is as if he (Sachs) had written the Prelude himself, and set up the terms in which the drama was going to be played out, a crucial factor being, as we discover in due course, that he is intent on manipulating things without anyone realising, at least until he has accomplished his work, that that is what he is doing. Furthermore, Wagner gives us a full-length portrait of Sachs in the profound Prelude to Act III, which is all the more moving because it has not been adumbrated, except in some of the contrapuntal complexities of Act II. All the other characters, as befits a comedy, are presented in their fullness on appearance. As soon as we see and hear them, we know them. Which is not to say that they are all simple, though most of them are (quite). The music gives them some complexity, thanks to Wagner's sovereign mastery by this stage of his career. So as soon as we encounter Pogner, Eva's father, we recognise him as a burgher of dignity, kindness, pride and determination. Walther is instantly the headstrong young aristocrat, haughty and vulnerable. And so on.

But Sachs is someone whom we get to know only gradually. In Act I he is often hardly noticed, his interjections in the meeting of the Masters are so unassertive, though he is intent on making his points. But he gets to know himself only gradually, too. At the end of Act I he is left on stage alone, scratching his head in bemusement, not yet sure how he can order events. And it is clear from the confusion in which the act ends that he is going to have to be a master-strategist. For Walther has made a fool of himself with the Masters, and it is difficult to see how he can even take part in the Song Contest the next day, a necessary condition for winning Eva's hand. Stung by their rejection, Walther is liable to ignore their rules even more comprehensively, though he is determined to gain the prize, just as Eva is determined to be gained by him. 'You or no one!' she cries after having known Walther for five minutes.

Early in Act II, after the wonderfully tender scene in which Eva and Pogner discuss the coming contest, both of them keeping their cards close to their chests, Sachs has the first of his monologues, and we find him meditative, impatient with his own shortcomings, susceptible to the new in art – most of the monologue involves his trying to capture the song which earned the Masters' ridicule, and finally succeeding – and deeply understanding of the nature of Walther's talent: 'nun sang er, wie er musst'; und wie er musst', so konnt' er's' (he sang as he had to, and as he had to, so he could). He realises, too, that because of the nature of Walther's talent, which is the genuine expression of his feelings, what he sang obeyed no rules, and yet was without fault. Equally, since Walther sang of familiar states of mind in fresh ways, because the states are fresh for him, 'Es klang so alt, und war doch so neu' (It sounded so old, and yet was so new). And Sachs's reflections here contain several references to birdsong; yet he knows that a bird doesn't produce art, so that to the extent that Walther takes birds as his model (and has been taunted for doing so in Act I), he needs to learn the difference.

What Sachs has to say about Walther's song is also what

he feels about Walther himself: *Die Meistersinger* is, more than anything else, about the connections between life and art, between individuals' lives and the art they produce, and between the life of a community and its attitude to art. Walther's art is glamorous, impetuous, passionate and (so far) undisciplined, all qualities that it almost too obviously shares with the man himself. Though Sachs alone among the Masters appreciates the positive qualities there, he is also aware (as the creator of *Tristan* surely was too) of the dangers involved. As he says to Walther during their long scene in Act III: 'Eu'r Lied hat [die Meister] bang' gemacht; und das mit Recht: denn wohl bedacht, mit solchem Dicht' – und liebesfeuer verführt man wohl Töchter zum Abenteuer; doch für liebseligen Ehe-stand man andre Wort und Weisen fand' (Your song made the Masters anxious, and with good reason: for if you think about it, it's with such fire of poetry and love that one seduces daughters to adventure; but for loving and blessed marriage other words and tunes must be found). This, it is clear, is an artist issuing a warning about the power of art. The tones in which Sachs expresses it are half-humorous, half-solemn. The solemnity is justified, because Walther almost did elope with Eva the previous night; and though she hasn't yet been exposed to his music-making (that will happen a few minutes later), since it is the unbridled expression of his personality, the chances are that she would succumb to it as readily as she did to him.

At a deeper level, and one which really concerned Wagner more, Sachs is stressing the importance of having more than one kind of art around. Walther can only see the value of his own kind, but that is because, as Sachs explains to him in one of the most touching parts of the score, anyone can sing in spring, in their time of youthful ardour. But after that come 'Kindtauf', Geschäfte, Zwist and Streit' (children, business, discord and strife), and the real test of a Master is whether he can make music out of *them*. Walther's reply, an ecstatic and impatient 'Ich lieb' ein Weib, und will es frei'n' (I love a woman, and want to have her), raises the emotional temperature in a way that vindicates Sachs's wisdom. But Wagner must have been thinking of more than the appropriateness of different works of art to advancing stages of life, since Sachs himself is susceptible to the ardour of Walther's song. A prosy distillation of Sachs's reflections, throughout the drama, on art might run like this: art is an illusion, like everything else – he calls the Prize Song, in the preliminary version he has heard in his workshop, a 'selige[r] Morgentraum' (beautiful morning dream) – but it is a conscious illusion, and therefore won't mislead us into taking it for truth – or will it? It won't if we subject our immediate promptings to the discipline of tradition. (But what if it is aware of tradition in order to ignore it, the case of *Tristan*, once more, or of *Le Sacre du Printemps*?) If we fail to do that, the result will be intoxicating formlessness, which will defeat the whole purpose of art.

In other words, ones to be used sixty years later to make a related but separate point: there must be a balance between tradition and the individual talent. The Masters have succumbed to the danger of prizing tradition at the expense of the new; Walther is contemptuous of rules, because for him spontaneity is everything. And in the wings, as it were, there are Beckmesser and David, the former perhaps once just like the latter now is – and a warning for David of what he might become. David is so enraptured by his own success in having learned the rules that he uses them to show off, precisely the wrong use of tradition, and the recipe for being the worst kind of teacher, as Wagner shows that he is in Act I. Beckmesser too is a prisoner of the rules, and so when he has genuine emotion to express, as in his wooing of Eva in Act II, the result is a comprehensive mess, in which the rules are misapplied and the emotion becomes ridiculous.

Sachs, as the voice of his creator, realises all this, understands the conditions for genuine creation, and therefore wouldn't attempt a Prize Song himself. For the object of the Prize Song is not only to demonstrate mastery of tradition, but also to win Eva's hand: one must take account not only of how to compose, but of what the composition is for. And Eva is not for him: he has to renounce her, and therefore contents himself, when he is in songful mood, with singing his cobbling songs, which serve more than one purpose – in Act II to keep Beckmesser quiet, in Act III to conceal his emotions by turning his song into a more than half-serious complaint – and thus show, once more, that art has various roles to play in relation to life.

How easy it is to miss, or overshoot, the mark had in fact been made very clear to Sachs the previous night. For his cobbling song, designed successfully to put Beckmesser off, and also to prevent Eva from eloping with Walther, had triggered off a scene of ugly violence, in which Beckmesser was beaten up, and the citizens of Nürnberg in general showed themselves in a bad light. It is that which leads to the greatest of Sachs's monologues, on the subject of 'Wahn', the next morning, near the opening of Act III. The Prelude to that act has begun with the theme usually called 'Sachs's resignation' on the gloomy lower strings, and as it is taken up and developed contrapuntally we get a sense of the depth and pain of his reflections. But these musings give way, with noble effect, to the melody which will be the hymn with which the populace greets him on the Festival Meadow later in the day: intoned softly by the brass, it conveys the wealth of emotion which exists between Sachs and the community. Then his cobbling song, his signature tune, as it were, is breathed out by the strings, in a gentle, hesitating form, and ascends to the heights, 'very tenderly and expressively', spinning itself out to reveal the warmth at the centre of Sachs's character. The chorale enters again, reaching a resplendent climax; and finally the massed strings break in angrily, or tormentedly, to stress how all Sachs's wisdom is founded in his suffering. It is a complete portrayal of a complex person such as Wagner had not attempted before, but would be doing again, in the next Prelude he wrote (to Act III of *Siegfried*).

The mood lightens, as it needs to, for the scene between David and his master, though it is punctuated by the Resignation theme, as indeed the whole act is. Then Sachs is left alone with his world chronicle, and he ponders on 'Wahn', a word that is the despair of translators, but which is located in the area marked out by 'illusion', 'folly', 'madness'. For Sachs it is the word which characterises everything, and which therefore seems to mark him out as a faithful Schopenhauerian *avant la lettre*. He begins, certainly, in very low spirits, only able to see 'Wahn' as a source of pain and evil – tearing their own flesh, people mistake their own cries for those of their neighbours whom they are mistreating (this is *echt*-Schopenhauer). His reflections along this line come to an abrupt end, as he finds himself completely at a loss. He turns, after a pause, to thinking about his beloved Nuremberg, peacefully basking in the centre of Germany. But that leads him back to reflecting on what happened last night, when things got hopelessly out of control (thanks to his song), and he is brought to another dead end. A bigger pause, and then magical music, suggesting another midsummer night – but that was a dream, and Sachs's was not – leads him to whimsical explanations of how such things can happen: no other kind of explanation will do. This is the grand moment, referred to earlier, when night gives way to day, and Sachs has his moment of deepest insight into what he, as an artist, must do: 'Jetzt schau'n wir, wie Hans Sachs es macht, dass er den Wahn fein lenken kann, ein edler Werk zu tun; denn lässt er uns nicht ruh'n, selbst hier in Nürnberg, so sei's um solche Werk', die selten vor gemeinen Dingen, und nie ohn' ein'gen Wahn gelingen' (Now let's see how Hans Sachs can manage things so that 'Wahn' can be made to do nobler work; for if it will not let us rest even here in Nuremberg, then let it be in the service of such works which seldom arise from ordinary things, and never succeed without a touch of 'Wahn'). This astonishing mouthful is set to music of transporting rapture, which Wagner can't possibly have thought would do anything to make his elaborate thought, and its contorted expression, easier to follow. But when one scrutinises it at home, it becomes clear that Sachs has moved from Schopenhauer to late Nietzsche, again *avant la lettre*, this time on Wagner's part too. In *Twilight of the Idols* (German title: *Götzendämmerung*) Nietzsche presents a hilarious six-part account, in one page, of the history of Western thought, the last stage of which is as follows: 'The true world we have abolished. What world has remained? The apparent one perhaps? But no! *With the true world we have abolished the apparent one*' (Nietzsche's italics). Thus Sachs has realised that everything is 'Wahn', that there is no getting round it or beyond it. So if there is to be positive value in the world, as well as ineliminable evil, that will be by ingenious manipulation of illusion, not by its replacement by truth, or reality. Optimism can only, but it can, be cultivated within the framework of pessimism.

This is only the most blatant indication, perhaps, of the strange relationship that has developed by this point between Sachs and Wagner. In one way it seems that they are the same, and it hardly needs adding that Wagner has often been accused of both glamourising himself as the noble renouncer, and of identifying with Walther too, so that he both has his Eva and grandly forgoes her.

That seems to me uninteresting. The vital question, more taxing than this piece of pseudo-biographical impudence, is that of whether we can get any perspective on Sachs, or whether we are back yet again with the figure Wagner wanted to escape, but that the intensity of his successive convictions kept on forcing him to create: the 'absolute artist'. That Sachs is almost wholly sympathetic, the most completely sympathetic character Wagner created, is not the point at issue either. It is whether he is invested with an authority, or a kind of authority, which takes him out of the framework of the drama, and allows him to play god. Well, he does take it upon himself to get two potential disasters averted: he has to make sure that Beckmesser is discredited, and he has to get Walther admitted as a competitor in the contest even though he doesn't have the Masters' required credentials. The methods he adopts to bring those results about show that he is a man who believes that the ends justify the means. He is happy to let Beckmesser claim the text of the Prize Song as his own, knowing that he will make a hash of it, thereby provoking him to claim that the words were by Sachs, a charge which can only be refuted by letting the genuine author step forth and show what the Song is really like.

But though he plans and executes Walther's success by getting everyone to play to his tune, while rather boorishly complaining that no one does, Sachs gives no indication at any stage that he is all-knowing. It is rather his devotion to Eva and his affection for Walther which motivate him, and his rejection of the role of King Marke, already referred to, shows that he is acting out of self-interest as well as concern for the young pair. Though he makes light of the reference to the 'sad tale' of Tristan and Isolde, it is actually a pivotal moment in the action. For Eva has been, under the stress first of Walther's singing of his Song, and second of Sachs's ironic tirade, shaping up to see herself as an Isolde-figure, for which she has neither the right kind of voice nor the right temperament. Her outburst 'O Sachs! Mein Freund!' is both a cry from the heart and a piece of self-dramatisation. When Sachs cuts her off, to the accompaniment of *Tristan's* yearning motif, the effect is of recoil: 'For Heaven's sake, not that!' Sachs is rejecting both the role of King Marke and the whole ethos in which being Marke is a possibility. That is made clear by the brevity of his reply, before the orchestra enters in top *Meistersinger* form. Eva's brief flirtation with the metaphysics of transcendent love – she would choose Sachs, she sings, if she *had* any choice, but she is in the grip of 'ein Müssen ... ein Zwang' (a 'must', a compulsion), and is destined 'zu nie gekannter Qual' (for never-known anguish) – is conclusively scotched by Sachs. She is clearly overdoing things, and by the time she opens her mouth again it is to launch the Quintet, which really is an unaffected utterance, and the deepest she can give voice to.

Sachs, then, for all his authority and decisiveness, is no Prospero or Sarastro; what he does is done on the basis of what he knows, and the consequences vindicate him. And while he is the drama's central figure, and certainly its most interesting one – Walther, apart from his musical gifts, is nothing special, and Eva is ideally suited to him – he is still dependent on the community in which he lives not only for his livelihood, a comparatively humble one, but also for his status. The crowd are perfectly prepared to question him after Beckmesser's indictment. If Wagner were any closer to him than he is, we would feel unease. Some people do anyway, but that is because they have failed to observe the subtle touches which Wagner employs to indicate Sachs's fallibility. Further, by excluding him from the Overture, Wagner shows that there is plenty of exuberant life without Sachs, that he is a contingent element in the drama, however important to its outcome.

So the complexity of *Die Meistersinger* might be put, almost diagrammatically, as follows: the essence of the world is 'Wahn', but most people, being fully in thrall to it, don't realise that. So they are happy or miserable, but with no comprehensive view of what those states come to, or why they are in them. Since it is anyway not the kind of knowledge that most people could make any use of, that is a good thing – and so *Die Meistersinger* is a comedy. Sachs has the knowledge, it saddens him, but it doesn't incapacitate him. The likelihood of things going wrong rather than right is sufficiently great for him to have no high estimate of the possibilities of life in general – so at the level of true insight, *Die Meistersinger* is pessimistic, though not tragic. But sometimes it is possible for a sufficiently wise person to involve himself in events to good purpose, so long as he keeps some distance from the passions at the centre of them. Sachs seizes the opportunity when it comes, things work out as he planned, so *Die Meistersinger* is a comedy in the end, as well as in the beginning. It is the intrusive central layer that is so moving and fascinating, and which gives the work its depth.

13

The *Ring* Resumed

When Wagner resumed work on the *Ring* in 1869, after twelve years, he was a very different artist, and so a very different person, from the one who had left Siegfried following the Woodbird. The *Ring* had been conceived, in its full version, as a conspectus of human society, seen from a mythic point of view, in which the rule of the gods was eventually to be replaced by human beings governed by love. But we saw that at the end of Act II of *Siegfried* Wagner had grown weary of tracing his hero's slow ascent to love, and abandoned him so that he could work out what love might be in a work in which it constituted the sole reality. When it took on those ontological pretensions, though, it turned out to be a very different affair from any that the *Ring* had envisaged. There could be no question of love governing a race of people, because only the death-devoted pair were up to its demands. Love in this shape obliterates the world. Which meant that from now on Wagner would have to keep two concepts of love going, one of the *Tristan* variety, the other the concept which would be operative in the remainder of the *Ring*. What would such a concept be, other than a banal one which didn't need the largest drama ever composed to define it?

Meanwhile, and to complicate matters further, Wagner had dealt with a full-blooded society in *Die Meistersinger*, and one which though it was not in an obvious way mythic, was not in any serious sense historic either. In that society love, as evidenced in the relationship of Walther and Eva, was the usual kind of thing which leads to marriage, children, and with any luck middle-aged companionship. The more fundamental truths of *Die Meistersinger* had to do with issues unconnected with love. Was there something missing from Wagner's vision there, that he needed to return to the Herculean effort of composing Act III of *Siegfried* and the whole of *Götterdäm-merung*? Evidently he thought that there was, but it must have been a question for him what the substance of these works was now to be. Of course the texts were there to be set, but by this time the whole import of words and action could be changed by the musical powers at his disposal, and it is clear that it was they that Wagner was looking to to provide him with his answers, and up to a point the problems to which they were answers.

Wagner's most helpful comments on the *Ring*, which we needn't take as definitive of its meaning, but should be respect-ful towards, were to his revolutionary friend August Röckel, who had not been as fortunate as Wagner in escaping after the failure of the Dresden uprising in 1849, but spent thirteen years in prison. Wagner kept him informed of his progress on the *Ring*, and did his best to answer Röckel's often searching questions about it. In the course of his longest letter to Röckel, dated 25/26 January 1854, Wagner writes: 'Wodan [as he was still called at this stage] rises to the tragic heights of *willing* his own destruction. This is all we need to learn from the history of mankind: *to will what is necessary* and to bring it about ourselves. The final creative product of this supreme, self-destructive will is a *fearless* human being who never ceases to love: Siegfried.' One's first reaction to the last sentence of this extract is to wonder when Siegfried is going to *begin* to love. Not that he has had any opportunities yet, but hasn't an inordinate time been occupied with his doing things which are not of ultimate importance for his destiny? At any rate, if the Woodbird is to be trusted, the occasion for love will soon arise. But there is still one major obstacle in his path: Wotan, his grandfather and the agent of his father's death, so far not intervening in events in Siegfried's opera, but getting ready for his last stand.

Wagner leaves us in no doubt of his full commitment to the *Ring* in the Prelude to Act III, the most imposing and complex piece of orchestral writing yet in the cycle. It is, as the Prelude to Act III of *Die Meistersinger* had been, a portrayal of the character who is about to appear. Motifs conceived many years before are now heard in a rich, intense counterpoint which shows the state of mind of the god as he approaches his final confrontations. Though it sounds nothing like any of the music in the two dramas that had interposed, it could never have been written without them. The god of *Das Rheingold* seems a faint memory, and even the Wotan of *Die Walküre* was not as multi-layered as the Wanderer, previously in *Siegfried* sustained by a single melody of sonorous grandeur, is now evidently to be. When the curtain rises, he sweeps in to invoke Erda, needing to learn from her what the future will be. She is unwilling, and in any case unable, to give him any answers, and they end in mutual recriminations. But her taunts give him an opportunity to express himself at length on the difference between the god she knew and the one she is now refusing to help. 'Weisst du, was Wotan will?' (Do you know what Wotan wills?) he asks her, with a long silence after, which reminds us of his stricken willing of 'Das Ende!' in his monologue in *Die Walküre*. This time, however, instead of a bitter blessing on Alberich's son, he launches into a radiant welcome to the man who will displace him: 'Was jene auch wirken, dem ewig Jungen weicht in Wonne der Gott' (Whatever will happen, to one who is eternally young the god now gladly yields), he sings, inspired as he has never been before. And with that Erda, whom Wotan unkindly calls 'Ursorge' (Primal care), sinks back, and the Wanderer prepares for his meeting with Siegfried, who is just coming into view.

Their meeting is at first poignant and funny, then a furious conflict of wills, and ends in the Wanderer's swift disappearance from the scene, and from the cycle, in a Sophoclean moment. While the Wanderer is eager to talk, Siegfried is only interested in getting to Brünnhilde, so gives short shrift to the jovial but, as he sees them, condescending questions of the old man – and he has had enough of old men, small or large. Reversing the outcome of the scene at the end of Act II of *Die Walküre*, he shatters Wotan's spear with the reforged Nothung, notices the increasing glow of the flames on the mountain-top, and, playing his horn, plunges fearlessly into them, to find himself on top of the world, confronted by a sleeping, recumbent figure and a horse, also asleep, nearby. The long solo passage in which he attempts to awaken Brünnhilde, succeeding only when he has kissed her, encouragingly shows new sides to his nature. Finally she sits up, greets the earth and sky in solemn tones, and has to begin her painful journey to acceptance of the fact that she is no longer a goddess. The psychological penetration of this scene, so far as she is concerned, is one of the *Ring*'s high points. But the fact that there is so much psychology shows what a non-mythological being Brünnhilde has now become. Siegfried, in love at first sight, is in no position to offer her insights into her predicament, so can only give her enthusiastic backing as she comes gradually to terms with her new status. The scene moves slowly into top gear, as each of them is overcome with desire for the other, and it notoriously ends with expressions of frenzied ardour so noisy and unabashed that many listeners are still shocked. Really the most shocking thing about them is their final words: 'leuchtende Liebe, lachender Tod!' (light-giving love, laughing death!). Does that indicate that they are in such an advanced state of excitement that they are prepared to sing anything, or should we pay special attention to the fact that they are singing that? To judge from Wagner's letter to Röckel, the same one from which I quoted earlier, the latter is what he intended.

In the course of that letter, Wagner writes: 'We must learn *to die*, and *to die* in the fullest sense of the word; fear of the end is the source of all lovelessness, and this fear is generated only when love itself is beginning to wane. How did it come about that a feeling which imparts the highest bliss to all living things was so far lost sight of by the human race that everything that the latter did, ordered and established was finally conceived only out of fear of the end? My poem shows the reason why.' Clearly Wagner set himself an agenda that was as ambitious as it was magnificent. Or at least, that is what he claimed to have done. He seems to have been reading the poem of the *Ring* and imparting new meanings to it, for nowhere in the text is there reference to fear of death as the root of all evil. What one increasingly comes to feel as one sees, hears and studies the *Ring* is that Wagner told a riveting and complicated story in it, leaving it open to multiple interpretations, which the music if anything adds possibilities to, rather than, as Wagner often claimed, 'making everything clear'. That is not to say that it is wholly indeterminate in meaning, but that it is, like life itself, indefinitely discussable, though during the course of discussion some accounts of what it means will be abandoned, others strike one as exceptionally apt. The reflections which the characters, especially Wotan, indulge in are part of the data which we have to make sense of. As Wagner puts it later in the same letter, 'I believe that it was a true instinct that led me to guard against an excessive eagerness to make things plain, for I have learned to feel that to make one's intentions too obvious risks impairing a proper understanding of the work in question; in drama – as in any work of art –, it is a question of making an impression not by parading one's opinions but by setting forth what is instinctive.'

Yes, but what about the course that we find the *Ring* taking? Act III of *Siegfried* is decisive in every way. It does, and very movingly, show Wotan embracing his own eclipse, though he has no immediate prospects of, or plans for, dying. He has never had a fear of the end, so far as we know, only a fear of being subservient to anyone else. He is happy, it seems from his colloquy with Erda, to retire to Valhalla and leave the rest of the world to go on its way, certain that things will be in the safe hands of the 'eternally young'. His last-ditch resistance to Siegfried is especially touching, showing us that the old Wotan does still exist, and is not prepared to listen to an insult unresistingly. It may be, too, that he wants to assure himself that Siegfried really is all he hopes, by seeing whether his sword is stronger than Wotan's own spear – with the rules by which he has governed the world engraved on it, and so now presumably vanquished as he is. He must be satisfied by the degree of ignorance that Siegfried shows, since that still remains a necessary condition for righting the wrongs which Wotan committed.

The huge significance of Siegfried's awakening of Brünnhilde is indicated by the music to which she wakes up, by some way the most exalted that we have heard in the *Ring*. It combines solemnity with ecstasy in a way that Wagner made his own. The duet moves from the mindless rapture of the opening few minutes, through Brünnhilde's fear of giving herself to a man, even this man, to a realisation that it is by becoming human that she can gain a happiness that for all her Walküre yodelling she could never have attained as a goddess.

This is the counterpart to her experience of compassion in her confrontation with Siegmund, where she wonderingly came to see what human love meant in terms of the sacrifices human beings would make for one another. Having been awoken, in every sense, by Siegfried, she can combine the recklessness of her former life, heroic in its simultaneous defiance and embracing of death, with the tenderness and vulnerability which she had witnessed in Siegfried's father and mother.

Exciting and convincing as all this is, one might reflect that it does show a sharp narrowing of focus. Even Wotan's scenes, heavy with mythic significance, especially with the elaborate and allusive musical texture in which they are embedded, has our interest directed more on his personal fate than on that of the world over which he ruled. And Siegfried and Brünn-hilde show no interest in anyone other than themselves and one another. Wotan is absorbed in his own drama of renunci-ation, Siegfried and Brünnhilde in becoming lovers. And all this is leading up to the cosmic drama of *Götterdämmerung*. How?

Wagner shows how with the opening two chords of *Götter-dämmerung*, a subtle but overwhelming modification of the chords to which Brünnhilde awoke. They are so doom-laden that we can have no doubt about the range of their significance. And the scene of the Three Norns confirms our apprehension. They tell us a great deal that we didn't know before, crucially about Wotan's early activities, which occurred well before the opening of *Das Rheingold*. In a sense, then, we are at the beginning again, but this time with an understanding which we didn't have when the cycle started of what is at stake. But this is plainly, thanks to the interweaving of the remote past and the immediate future in what the Norns communicate, the beginning of the end. Like Erda, their wisdom is at an end, as is everything connected with the gods, and their rope of Fate snaps, so they sink powerless back to join Erda in timeless, pointless sleep.

The orchestral passage which succeeds the Norns' disappearance shows Wagner's art of transition, the art of which he was proudest, at its most superb. Siegfried's horn-call has been transformed into the proud motif of Siegfried as hero, and Brünnhilde is now voluptuously feminine, their motifs first alternating, then intertwining as dawn breaks, and they enter in the highest spirits. ('*Dämmerung*' means both 'dusk' and 'dawn', and the Norns have prefigured the dusk of the gods, and also, it seems, the dawn of mankind.) Brünnhilde is keen that Siegfried should set off on new adventures, now that she has imparted to him all her wisdom. Siegfried fears, all too plausibly, that he has not been an apt pupil, but nothing stems their full-blown, fully human passion (not a hint of any Tristanesque quality), and they end by telling the gods to look down on them and feast their eyes. This duet needs to be savoured to the utmost, since there is very little to be joyful about afterwards.

Siegfried arrives in the land where men and women are scheming and insecure, willing to do anything to shore up their constantly flagging self-esteem – the introduction of a set of new characters at this stage (they survive, of course, from Wagner's first plans for the *Ring*) is managed with masterly economy. The figure at the centre of the action is that son of Alberich's, Hagen, whom Wotan had blessed in his bitter monologue in Act II of *Die Walküre*. Acting apparently on his father's behalf, he has plans for getting the Ring, which Siegfried, unaware of its (alleged) properties, has left with Brünnhilde as a love-token. With the help of a potion Siegfried forgets Brünnhilde (this rather clumsy device can best be taken as Wagner's way of compressing Siegfried's absorption into the world of intrigue, which is effected all the sooner because he is without suspicion) and falls for Gutrune, Hagen's half-sister.

The squalors of this scene are so brutally at odds with what has gone before that one can only wish that Siegfried and Brünnhilde had remained in happy domesticity on her rock. Their love certainly turns out to be fragile, needing a barrier from reality. That is what it plainly is for Brünnhilde. For while Siegfried is away she is visited by one of her sister Walküren, Waltraute, who comes to bring her up to date about Wotan's plight. The god, with his shattered spear in his hand, sits silently waiting for the end. If only Brünnhilde would give back to the Rhinemaidens their Gold, 'von des Fluches Last erlös't wär Gott und Welt' (from the weight of the curse both god and world would be saved). Is there a hint, retained by Wagner, that if the Ring were returned then the gods might live happily ever after? It seems odd if there is, but obscure if there isn't.

Waltraute's words are incomprehensible to Brünnhilde. In a passage which shows the exultant egoism of love, she tells her sister to report to Wotan that 'die Liebe liesse ich nie' (I will never relinquish love), and certainly not the Ring. It is a hideous irony that the Ring, which is the symbol of the renunciation of love, is here treated as love's guarantee, especially in the light of what will soon be happening. Waltraute's narration is one of the most moving passages in the whole cycle, and makes Wotan as real a presence as he would be if he were on stage. That it should fall on deaf ears is surely a critique of what becomes of people in love – and Wagner always insisted that the basic form of love was sexual. Nor does it give Brünnhilde strength when the rock is invaded by Siegfried disguised as Gutrune's brother Gunther, and failing, in his drugged state, to recognise his beloved.

By this stage we are puzzled as to what love might come to,

if it is more than the familiar kind we saw in *Die Meistersinger*, and less than the wholly transcendent love of Tristan and Isolde. The answer seems to be that there is no room for a further kind, fortifying and world-redeeming. That, at any rate, is the conclusion that Wagner himself came to when he was working on the *Ring*, so that its message becomes a progressively pessimistic one: there is no general recipe for making the world less grievously unsatisfactory than it is.

This conclusion was forced on him by reflecting on the closing scene of *Götterdämmerung*, a great peroration for Brünnhilde – but what is she to say that can even appear to redeem the situation? This problem plagued Wagner for years. He wrote for her these words (among many others): 'Nicht Gut, nicht Gold, noch göttliche Pracht; nicht Haus, nicht Hof, noch herrischer Prunk: nicht trüber Verträge trügender Bund, noch heuchelnder Sitte hartes Gesetz: selig in Lust und Leid lässt – die Liebe nur sein!' (Not wealth, nor gold, nor godly pomp; not house, not hearth, nor lordly splendour; not troubled treaties' treacherous bonds, not smooth-tongued custom's hard decree: blessed in joy and sorrow – there is only love!). Apart from their miserable poetic quality, far inferior to the staple of Wagner's verse, which may be what strikes us most forcefully, these lines struck Wagner, he told Röckel in a letter of 1856, as 'tendentious'. And he continues, astonishingly: 'I had (unfortunately!) never really sorted out in my own mind what I meant by this "love" which, in the course of the myth, we saw as something utterly and completely destructive.'

This candid admission that what had seemed to be the great positive value of the *Ring* is 'utterly destructive' leaves us pondering what the shape of the work, what its direction, really is.

But though Wagner cut that embarrassing passage, he

didn't alter Brünnhilde's last words, which she sings as she rides into Siegfried's funeral pyre, after she has sung his praises, having found out that he was the victim of Hagen's deceit; and having forgiven Wotan for causing all the trouble in the first place, and pronounced her sublime benediction on him: 'Ruhe, ruhe, du Gott!' (Rest, rest, thou god!). She has promised the Rhinemaidens, too, that they will at last have their Gold returned to them, so it remains only for her to perform the sacrificial act which will set the world to rights. As climax is piled on climax, she mounts Grane, and sings 'ihn zu umschlingen, umschlossen von ihm in mächtigster Minne, vermählt ihm zu sein! Heiajoho! Grane! Grüss deinen Herren! Siegfried! Siegfried! Sieh'! Selig grüsst dich dein Weib!' (to embrace him, embraced by him in highest love, to be wedded to him! Heiayoho! Grane! Greet your master! Siegfried! Siegfried! See! Blessedly your wife greets you!).

This whole scene is on a level of inspiration which enables Wagner at least to give the impression that all the threads of the *Ring* have been drawn together, and that in her great-heartedness and complete understanding Brünnhilde has achieved a purging synthesis; because that is what the music undoubtedly achieves. So that other kind of synthesis, desiderated by the intellect, is for the time being not something it would be possible to seek. But look at Brünnhilde's words: like Isolde, she is in a state of advanced delusion. She will not be embraced by Siegfried, because he is dead, and there will be no Valhalla for them to go to, since in a moment it will be going up in flames. And she does revert to the subject of love, even to marriage. This is where Wagner is most triumphant, and most vulnerable. By this stage in his career his capacity for writing huge stretches of music of incessant exaltation means that he could, if he pleased, seduce us into accepting anything. And when one looks at the end of *Götterdämmerung* it seems that that is what he has done. After Brünnhilde leaps, the final five minutes are, if anything, more powerful still. The Rhine overflows, Hagen has the last word (literally) as he tries to get the Ring, but is drowned by the Rhinemaidens, and then, as Flosshilde holds it aloft we see Valhalla being consumed by fire. Meanwhile, once the Rhine has subsided, the orchestra quietly plays the Rhinemaidens' theme, then that of Valhalla, and floating above on the violins the theme that has not been heard since Act II of *Die Walküre*, and which has usually been miscalled 'Redemption through love'. If it needs a title at all, it should be, Wagner said, 'the glorification of Brünnhilde', which would suit both occasions of its use. The *Ring* ends with it, too, after Siegfried's motif has been heard for the last time, and that of the downfall of the gods. But whatever its specific connotations, it is both consolatory and suggests a promise, though we can have no clear idea what it is a promise of.

There has been debate about the ending of the *Ring* since it was first performed; indeed, as we have seen, since it was first conceived. It was originally to end quite differently, with Brünnhilde leading Siegfried up to Valhalla, and obviously what she sings in the final version shows traces of that. But Wagner decided early on that the gods must perish. In the 1854 letter to Röckel he wrote: 'Instead of the words: "a gloomy day dawns on the gods: in shame shall end your noble race, if you do not give up the Ring!" I now make *Erda* say merely: "All that is – ends; a gloomy day dawns on the gods: I counsel you, shun the Ring!"' and then continues about fear of the end being the cause of all lovelessness. So Wagner determined that the gods should perish even if the Ring were returned to the Rhine, a frequent source of worry to those who try to make comprehensive sense of the *Ring*. It seems that his idea became that Wotan should at least regain his moral position, so far as that was possible, and that he should also will, because it was still a compromise – he would not have shed his guilt – that he should perish, thereby revealing that the death of the 'immortal gods' holds no terrors for him. His hopes for a world over which he didn't preside were doomed to disappointment, because like his creator he failed to see the destructive force inherent in love.

That is something that Brünnhilde never, it seems, learns. 'Alles weiss ich: alles ward mir nun frei!' (All things I know, all is clear to me now), she sings in her final musings. But it seems that she is mistaken. That may be the price of ecstasy, as it was for Isolde. Our most valued states of consciousness are not ones in which we are most closely related to truth. That is a shock for Western man, indoctrinated by Plato and Christ with the view that only apprehension and love of truth can give us those extreme states of bliss for which we crave, or at any rate can give them to us in lasting form. Wagner, brought up in this tradition and very much hoping it was right, explored every avenue he could find to confirm that it was. As one after another failed him, he came to show characters *expiring* in ecstasy – the best way to go. And there is a rank among delusions, established by criteria that may be as exigent as truth, though they will necessarily be very different. Wagner's criteria, repeated in one work after another, crucially involved making exorbitant demands on life, so that his central characters tend to oscillate between exaltation and exhaustion. 'Nirgends, ach nirgends find' ich Ruh'!' (Nowhere, ah nowhere shall I find peace!) Tristan cries in Act III; but is peace what he really wants? In a sense it is, but only the peace which comes from exhausting oneself in intensities of living. Wagner's characters are never prepared to die until they have deployed all the life within them. And there is no character with more superabundant life in her than Brünnhilde. To die on any other terms than a union with Siegfried, who had apparently betrayed her, whose death she had plotted, and whom she then discovered to have been innocent, is literally not in her power, and certainly not in her imagination. Would we be more moved by her if it were? I can't think so. Even, then, if love, as seen in the *Ring*, is 'something utterly and completely, destructive', what is there which is utterly and completely creative? Wagner had, at that stage, and until his final work, no answer, and neither do we. The 'sanity' of *Die Meistersinger* is wonderful, 'the C Major of this life' as Browning put it. But some of us want to modulate quite often, and into remote keys; and even then, such is our greed, to be chromatic. In which case we take risks, exploring strange regions of disharmony. But at the end of the *Ring*, as of Wagner's other mature works, it is very hard not to think that they are worthwhile.

So what is the *Ring* really about? For one thing, it seems not to be about the power of the Ring, as announced in the opening scene, since no one who gets it derives any benefit from it. Its first owner is easily robbed, so that far from giving him world domination, it doesn't even afford him minimal protection. Once he has cursed it, it is only to be expected that its owners won't benefit from it, or that they will ultimately come to grief. Fafner, its inheritor after Wotan's very brief period of possession, is too stupid to do anything except lie on it, and it doesn't help him in his fight with Siegfried. Siegfried has no idea what its point is, even though the Wood-bird explicitly tells him. He is only too pleased to give it to Brünnhilde as token of their love, but it fails to protect her, though she certainly knows all about it. She tries to ward off Gunther/Siegfried with it, but in vain. So Siegfried has it back again, and in his enthralling narration in Act III of *Götterdäm-merung* merrily tells the assembled company what the Woodbird had told him. It is no good arguing that the Ring lost its power after Alberich's curse, since that would convict the Woodbird of lying. Siegfried is, of course, not in the least interested in being 'lord of the world', but if he were interested it is hard to see how the Ring would help him. And yet it is what Alberich, making an eerie guest appearance at the beginning of Act II, and his son Hagen, are solely obsessed by.

Most people, it seems, spend the larger part of their lives pointlessly, doing nothing in particular or pursuing goals which will give them no satisfaction. The Ring is best seen, despite the Rhinemaidens' ill-advised claims on its behalf, as the image of what almost everyone seeks but either fails to find, or regrets it if they do. It is a focus, in the cycle, for extensive plotting, intrigue and deceit, but the only worth-while states we see anyone in are ones which are quite unrelated to it. If that was what Wagner was 'instinctively' trying to express, then he was overwhelmingly successful. But he was trying to express much more than that, even if that was part of it (which we may doubt, but that hardly matters). The *Ring* is, and only partly on account of its dimensions, his most sustained attempt to portray the complexities of life, not omitting anything which plays a vital role. Since he was an extraordinarily complex person anyway, his preparedness to express, or rather his insistence on not suppressing, any element in his experience and awareness was bound to result in something that is, in endlessly fascinating respects, untidy. Since he was among the greatest composers, more interested in the symphonic than the operatic tradition which he inherited, the *Ring*'s musical structure was bound to be, in various ways, at odds with its dramatic content, seeming to give the latter a coherence which in its honesty it can't possess. The resulting dislocations are among the chief reasons for the work's perennial appeal. A promise of wholeness is held out by one part of it, and denied by another. It is difficult to envisage a time when we shall no longer want to explore the conflicts within it, for that would suggest that we no longer had them in ourselves.

When he wrote the last notes of *Götterdämmerung* Wagner wrote the date, as was his habit, and 'I shall say no more.' But he must have known that he would not rest there. He needed, in the light of all the enemies of order and harmony which he had tracked, to make one more attempt to see where value of an enduring kind, less ambitious than in some of his earlier works, might lie. He had used one myth after another to cast light on the torment of existence, as he always felt it to be. But he had never seriously explored the essence of Christianity, despite his allegiance to Feuerbach, whose most famous book is called that. To treat it as a subject for artistic investigation, rather than as something to be promulgated or – insofar as it is possible for anyone in the culture of the West – to be ignored, would indeed set a crown on his unremitting lifelong toil.

14

Redemption to the Redeemer

Difficult as it is to believe, *Parsifal*, Wagner's work of peace and conciliation, has been and remains the subject of even more bitter contention than any of his other works. For many people it casts a spell so potent that they are unable to take it as anything more than an *objet*, to be contemplated with awe and devoted incomprehension. For others it is the climax of a life of brilliant charlatanism, the emission of 'tragic grunts' (Nietzsche), still more offensive than anything which precedes them, because the subject-matter is one that many members of our culture care about as their supreme value. In his essay 'Art and Religion', written in 1880 when he was composing the music, Wagner begins: 'One could say that when religion becomes artificial, it remains for art to salvage the true essence of religion by perceiving its mythical symbols – which religion would have us believe to be the literal truth – only according to their figurative value, in order to make us see their profound, hidden truth through idealised representation.' Which does not mean that Wagner is advocating that we make a religion of art, but rather that when we see that the role which only a religion in the genuine sense can play is no longer to be fulfilled by anything, it is to art that we should turn for all that our now reduced expectations can be provided with.

That statement of Wagner's is more helpful in approaching *Parsifal* than his designation of the work as 'Ein Bühnenweih-festspiel' (A stage-consecrating festival drama). That way of categorising it is dangerous, and was really no more than an indication that it was to be distinguished from other contemporary theatrical productions than as a positive specification of its nature. Since Wagner first thought of composing a drama on this subject in 1845, when he was thirty-two, and returned to it intermittently over the years, it is helpful to begin by tracing some connections between it and his other mature works. He drew up a prose sketch of it in 1865, shortly after the first performance of *Tristan*, and that sketch is in most respects close to the drama as it finally emerged. But he was too preoccupied with finishing first *Die Meistersinger*, and then with writing the music for Act III of *Siegfried* and of *Götterdämmerung*, not to mention building the Bayreuth Festspielhaus and training the performers for the first production of the *Ring*, to give it much thought for the next eleven years. He had always claimed that his last work for the stage would be *Parsifal*, and the fact that its subject remained in his mind for more than half his life, returning to the forefront of his consciousness in relation to his other key projects, and at crucial junctures of his creative development, is worth bearing in mind. Thus he at one point thought of introducing Parsifal himself into the Third Act of *Tristan*, juxtaposing a figure dying of love with one who has renounced love. Wisely he gave that idea up, but the subject continued to crop up during the writing of *Tristan*, and he came to feel that there was a strong connection between the character of Tristan and that of Amfortas, the head of the Knights of the Grail, who lost the sacred spear which pierced Christ's side to the black magician Klingsor as he lay helplessly in the arms of the seductress Kundry. Writing to Mathilde Wesendonck in May 1859, Wagner says what a frightful subject it would be: 'It suddenly became clear to me. Amfortas is my Third-Act Tristan inconceivably intensified.' One might have thought that any intensification of his Third-Act Tristan was inconceivable. Wagner goes on to explain the source of Amfortas's suffering, so vividly that he concludes this part of the letter with: 'And you expect me to carry through something like this? And set it to music, into the bargain? – No, thank you very much! I leave it to anyone who has a mind for such things; I shall do all I can to keep my distance from it.' But one of the reasons why he couldn't is made clear by his account of Amfortas's pains: they are not the pains of love itself, but of the consequences of having yielded to love, giving up everything else which he cared about in its interests, with disastrous results for the community which depends on him.

As he was composing the work – a process which is recorded from day to day in Cosima's diary – Wagner obsessively made connections between the characters in *Parsifal* and those in his other works. But even if we lacked that detailed testimony, many of these crucial correspondences would be clear. All his creative life long, Wagner was preoccupied, as we have often seen, with people who had no past – innocents, ignoramuses – and with people who had all too much of a past, who were burdened with having done something so dreadful (which might simply be having been born) that only by a prodigious act on their part, or on someone else's on their behalf, could they be released from the torments of an insupportable existence which could not be ended until they were absolved. In the first class the most obvious members are Siegfried and Walther. In the second and larger class are the Dutchman, Tannhäuser, Tristan and Wotan. Each class has its culmination in *Parsifal*. The eponymous hero is, at his first entrance, the limiting case of naïveté and ignorance, combined with amnesia about what past he has had. Amfortas takes the second class to its furthest bounds.

Wagner's hopes for his suffering heroes reside either in

their entering into some relationship with the innocent, potentially heroic figures who will remove their burden of guilt, or in their redemption through the love of a self-sacrificing woman. But one way or another in all his works until *Parsifal*, things become more complicated than might have been hoped, or the nature of the redemption which is accomplished remains obscure. Even so, they do explore possibilities of living with a vigour and pertinacity which has few equals in art. But in doing that, the initial terms, the broad contrasts, take on a complexity which so candidly mirrors that of life that there is a danger that no progress will be made. Or the redemptive process involves so superhuman an endeavour on the part of one character, aided by puzzling metaphysical or quasi-religious machinery, that one is left uneasy about the feasibility of such feats.

It is Wagner's achievement in *Parsifal* to render the resolution both psychologically convincing and to set it in a context where the basic elements are the most extreme he ever imagined. There are two particularly striking connections with his earlier works, besides the relationship to *Tristan* already touched on. One is *Die Meistersinger*, in which Walther brings new creative vigour to a community which is not in anything like so desperate a condition as that of the Grail. The second is the *Ring*, where the heroic burden is shared between two figures, one of whom, Siegfried, all too convincingly buckles under the strain. The other, Brünnhilde, transcends the human condition, as we have seen, by delusion, and we wonder how she relates to us with our meaner, less nourishing delusions. She is, in all ways, a mythic figure; while Walther, even when aided by Sachs, rather worryingly combines the glamorous and the commonplace.

It is typical of Wagner's heroic male figures that they are and feel isolated, but until Parsifal they all think that the road to salvation, or at any rate completion, lies through one or another kind of union with a woman, and they all find one, even if she isn't quite what they expected. Lohengrin is the obvious exception, but we saw that his drama is somehow both superficial and confusing. Far from suffering an identity-crisis, he seems to suffer from the opposite complaint, and his self-sufficiency remains bewilderingly ambiguous. What he needs from Elsa is so much at odds with what she needs from him that the result can only be unenlightening disaster, with the music as a kind of sauce diverting us from the issues to which it should be adding piquancy.

Parsifal, unlike his son Lohengrin – but I'm sure that the relationship is a red herring – is not only not prepared (as his son is) to say what his name is, but doesn't know it. Gurnemanz, the moving, pervasive 'chorus' of the outer acts, asks him a series of ever more elementary questions on his arrival, gently but with growing exasperation, and all Parsifal can reply is, 'I had many names, but now I have forgotten all of them,' which is Wagnerian synecdoche for having had many experiences which meant nothing to him. Not that he has no personality – his motif, which interrupts the music with marked effect as he is brought in by the knights and squires, outraged at his killing of a swan, shows that he is of the genus Siegfried at his most untutored, entirely a child of Nature. His engaging first words are 'Im Fluge treff' ich, was fliegt!' (I shoot at anything that flies!). Yet he can soon be made to feel guilt, even though he had no idea that he was doing anything wrong in shooting the swan.

It is this capacity for feeling pain, specifically at wrongdoing, whether his own or someone else's, which enables Parsifal to be the saving figure he eventually becomes. He has to answer to the prophecy which had gradually been expounded in the earlier part of Act I: 'Durch Mitleid wissend, der reine Tor'

(Knowing through pity, the pure fool). Each term of the prophecy is of equal weight. 'Fool' doesn't mean idiot, as Debussy maliciously said; he found the self-castrated magician Klingsor the only sympathetic figure in the drama, and was pleased to express his agreement with Klingsor's view of its hero. Both magician and musician underrate Parsifal: his folly is a condition of utter unawareness. 'Pure' qualifies this unawareness in the sense that becoming aware will not be for him, as it almost invariably is, a process of corruption. What is it about him which guarantees that, as he acquires knowledge, he won't be corrupted? His capacity for feeling with, so that 'pity' carries none of the connotations of condescension against which Nietzsche railed so effectively. So each element in the terse characterisation is not only equal, but interdependent. If Parsifal feels compassion, it will be by understanding pain, his own and/or someone else's. At the crucial moment, as we shall see, he won't make the distinction.

In Act I Parsifal doesn't get as far as that, but the ground is essentially prepared, and in two stages. First he is made to feel thoroughly ashamed of himself for having shot the swan, and for his instinctive violence towards Kundry when she tells him that his mother is dead. This is, as it were, a tenderising process, so that when in the Hall of the Grail he witnesses Amfortas's pain and anguish he convulsively clutches his heart. He has no idea what the pain means – indeed, it is primarily physical, and therefore means nothing. He is so bewildered by it that he can only shake his head and remain silent when Gurnemanz sharply asks him, 'Don't you know what you saw?' and pushes him angrily out of the side door. It is a revealing and slightly comic moment, this irascible behaviour on the part of one who has just received the Grail's blessing: a profoundly human touch on Wagner's part, to show the annoyance that unshared spiritual elevation often leads to, especially when hopes are high. The last word in the act goes to a voice from above, repeating the first part of the promise 'Made wise through pity, the pure fool', and further voices take it up and set the seal on it, 'Selig in Glauben' (Blessed in faith), a faith that Parsifal will perform the mission which he has begun so unpromisingly.

Wagner's powers as a dramatist of the most radically innovative kind are at their height in *Parsifal*, just as much in Act I, which sets up the terms of the action, as in the remaining acts. The Prelude, which excited Nietzsche to unexampled eloquence when he finally heard it in 1887, after years of *a priori* abuse, is a piece of scrupulous exposition which simultaneously contrives to offer the faintest hope of peace at the end of what is evidently going to be a long, excruciating journey. Its first section depicts what the drama will be centred around, the Grail which needs to be completed by the Spear – as figured by the long opening monody, a theme which can clearly be broken into parts, but somehow has to retain the integrity it tenuously possesses when we first hear it. No sooner have we heard this melody than we are shown how it can express devotion, agony, disintegration and fulfilment. Myth and psychology, that endlessly opposing but finally interdependent pair, are here manifest as one. The Prelude's middle section, alternating between softly breathing strings and sonorous brass, shows the state which the community needs to be in to be effective in its task. And the third section subjects the first to inquisition and torture, ending in, as Nietzsche put it, 'a look of love such as one finds expressed in Dante, nowhere else'.

The opening scene, in the lands of the Grail, succinctly lays before us the major elements: Gurnemanz and the young knights and squires at prayer, the arrival first of the wild and mysterious messenger Kundry, bringing balsam from Arabia, and then of the man who needs it so desperately, Amfortas, the wounded King. In some of his most exquisitely sensitive orchestration, Wagner depicts Nature here as the primary healer, the background against which the drama will be played out, but also a participant in it. As Amfortas is carried down to the lake for the washing of his wound, Gurnemanz explains to the young knights how the Grail got into such trouble, and what it was like before catastrophe overtook it: for the time being, happiness and wholeness can only be evoked as memory. And, as we saw, as soon as the promise of regained wholeness is voiced, it is only for it to be brutally interrupted by the arrival on the scene of a young barbarian.

After Parsifal has turned out to know nothing about any-thing, the orchestra quietly changes gear for what is known as the Transformation Music, during which he and Gurnemanz move to the Hall of the Grail, to music which, beginning as a march, the least expressive of musical forms, moves into counterpoint which seems to tear apart the very fabric of which it is composed, and climaxes in huge slabs of brass dissonance, an ultimate challenge to any kind of resolution, and flagellated by strings. This passage occupies a unique place in Wagner's *oeuvre*, and indeed in the history of music: pain which can only be conveyed in these terms takes art to the verge of the tolerable. And nothing that follows it, in the celebration of the sacrament, can do anything to assuage it, indeed can only sustain its intensity, as Amfortas makes all too vivid in his horrible cries for the 'Allerbarmer' (All-merciful One) to have mercy on him. Needless to say, the All-merciful One fails to oblige. If there is to be resolution, absolution, it will not come from on high.

Act II takes us into a different world – the land of the anti-Grail, Klingsor's domain. Here a suffering of a more revolting kind is at work, the suffering of someone who has given up hope and therefore wants to tear down the world. Whatever Amfortas's relation to Tristan, Klingsor is Alberich, but holding, it seems, the whip hand. Certainly in his scene with Kundry he manifests the power of malevolence and misery combined, fertilising one another so that Kundry, who can seduce anyone she has a mind to, can only be in bondage to a man who has renounced everything, even basic sensual pleasure, let alone love. Many other scenes in Wagner are agonising; this one is hateful. It makes the arrival of Parsifal all the more welcome: his entrance is similarly obtrusive to that in the First Act, but his motif is here expanded and doesn't end in disgrace. On the contrary, he is triumphant over Klingsor's knights, and this time the reproaches he receives swiftly give way to the seductive, lilting chorus of Flower-Maidens, Wagner's tribute to his adored Johann Strauss. That Parsifal is not even faintly tempted by them shows that he has yet to be awakened sexually, and it is for that purpose that Kundry, transformed into a bewitchingly lovely woman, is lying in wait.

The processes by which she attempts Parsifal's seduction are amazing in their resource and variety. The first stage is to re-animate Parsifal's sense of guilt, to make him loathe himself for his casual indifference to the mother he had left, thereby causing her death. Kundry's careful but voluptuous account of how he did that makes him vulnerable to an extreme degree, but this time, Kundry unwillingly hopes, to lust rather than pain. So when, in a moment of Freudian genius, she imparts his mother's dying greeting to him as love's first kiss – the turning point of the whole action, as is indicated by the extraordinarily disturbing music which accompanies that ambiguous kiss, vividly conveying both tumescence and a sense of revulsion – Kundry hopes that Parsifal, like many before him, will lie helpless in her arms.

Instead, what Parsifal feels is something, again physical,

which he immediately identifies with the pain of Amfortas
which he had witnessed uncomprehendingly in the Hall of
the Grail. But it takes him a little longer to realise that it is
not what he had first taken it for, a purely physical wound. It
is the 'Qual der Liebe' (torment of love) – that experience
which links him not only to Amfortas but also to Tannhäuser
and Tristan. In Tristan's last anguish he cries, 'Im Sterben
mich zu sehnen, vor Sehnsucht nicht zu sterben!' (To be
yearning in dying, but not to die of yearning!) – though it is
impossible to convey in English the equivocation of Tristan's
words, which make his fate so akin to Amfortas's, and thus by
transference to Parsifal's. The whole of *Tristan und Isolde* turns
on this equivocation, by which both the lovers, but he more
than she, see the essence of their being in yearning, so that
they crave death as the cessation of their torment, but at the
same time can't will that their love should cease, since it is the
only thing which they value. Parsifal, lacking the metaphysical
capacities of Tristan and Isolde, as well as the constitution
that necessitates their use, is not one to equivocate. He is
simply horrified at the effect that Kundry's kiss has on him,
and robustly calls his longing sinful – not something that
Tristan or Isolde would ever do, because they completely
bypass moral and theological categories.

Parsifal's rejection of the fever of love is so comprehensive
and convincing – and set to some of Wagner's subtlest music
– that Kundry realises that she had better try a different tack.
She tells Parsifal of the most appalling moment in her life, or
lives (*Parsifal* flirts with notions of reincarnation, at any rate
in Kundry's case) when she saw Christ - referred to only as
'Him' – as he passed by on the way to his crucifixion, and
laughed. He looked at her, and ever since she has been driven
from world to world, uncontrollably laughing, the momentary
expression of mirth changed into an eternity of hell. If Parsifal

pities Amfortas so much, what about her? She makes the astounding suggestion that he should spend one hour in her arms, which would redeem her – his purity is for her, in this demented state, a negotiable item.

Parsifal sees through that, and urges repentance on her. Kundry's brilliant riposte is to say that if he has learned so much merely by being kissed, how much more would he learn if they took things a good deal further. By now she is in thrall, unable to gain any perspective, to what Wagner has come to see at this stage as the 'utterly and completely destructive' power of love. Her view of Parsifal, in fact, amounts to a parody of love as redemption, though significantly it had always been the woman who had redeemed the man. When Parsifal says that only if she shows him the way to Amfortas will she be saved, she curses him vainly and calls on Klingsor's help. But Klingsor's prophecy at the start of the act – 'Only one who spurns you sets you free' – turns out, though it isn't immediately realised, to be true, and the act ends with Klingsor's magic garden destroyed and Parsifal setting out for the realm of the Grail.

I have recapitulated the action of Act II in a little detail because it is initially hard to follow, and Wagner leaves it strewn with ambiguities. Kundry, for instance, as the act proceeds, becomes increasingly confused about the relationship (or identity) between Christ and Parsifal. Actually there isn't one, but many listeners, impressed or nauseated, have followed in her wake. And though the psychology of the act is stunning in its depth and unflinching insight, its myth combines elements of both magic and religion in a way which leads one to uncertainty about the intrusion of the transcendent and mere conjuring tricks. To destroy Parsifal Klingsor hurls the Spear at him, but it hovers harmlessly above his head. Parsifal grasps it, makes the sign of the cross with it, and Klingsor's domain is obliterated. Wagner's penchant for bringing quite separate myths together and making them interact here exceeds itself, the whole point being – or this is the fundamental idea – that Parsifal can save others through saving himself. But Wagner had temporarily got into a jam in which a non-Christian and a Christian tale collide rather than colluding.

This act, so oddly different from those either side of it, and necessarily so, gives place to the most sustained serenity in Wagner's art. We endure the overwrought intensities of Act II in order to appreciate how hard-won, and convincing, the balm of Act III is. It only remains for Parsifal to accomplish his mission, having regained the Spear and thus acquired all the qualifications for redeeming Amfortas that were so painstakingly set out in Act I. But it turns out to be a big 'only'. Many years elapse between Acts II and III, as Parsifal, we gather, wanders lost, and the community of the Grail disintegrates without the daily sight of the holy vessel itself. Even so, it is clear from early on in Act III that everything will be put to rights, and it is Wagner's crowning achievement to produce a happy ending without forfeiting suspense, or leading us to wonder, as we so often do with happy endings, whether things really would have turned out so well. It is the reward of patience in this sublimely slow but sure music and drama that we have no such doubts. And the peace in which the work ends is one which mercifully is not that which passes understanding, but one which we have been able to grasp at every point as it comes into our view.

There can be few works which cut so deep and yet leave us feeling so intelligibly elevated. What, then, is the angry disputation which surrounds *Parsifal* about? Why does it become, if anything, ever more a centre of controversy as the years pass? Why – to be wholly explicit about it – are people not grateful for what Wagner has given them?

In the first place, Wagner's biography, which is repeated, with tiny modifications blown up into major revelations, as a kind of litany to render him as powerless as Klingsor, has him portrayed as increasingly monstrous towards the end of his life. At the time he was composing *Parsifal*, it is true that he was writing prose works which combine brilliance, crankiness and offensiveness to an extreme degree. He had become obsessed with the impurity of the German race, thanks to the infiltration of the Jews and the pollution of the blood through meat-eating, so, encouraged by Cosima, and overwhelmingly impressed by Gobineau's ludicrous theories of racial degeneration, he produced diatribes which make shocking reading. Commentators who hold gratifyingly simple views of the relationship between art and life cannot believe that opinions held so stridently can have failed to get into his works, especially *Parsifal*, which mentions blood quite often, though not the necessity for its being 'pure' – in fact it is bleeding rather than blood that the work is concerned with, a fairly clear distinction, one might have thought.

But many writers, of whom Robert Gutman in the United States and Hartmut Zelinsky in Munich are the most vociferous, see *Parsifal* as a myth of racial regeneration, with the Knights of the Grail as an endangered Aryan species and Kundry and Klingsor as corrupting Jews. Klingsor, after all, castrated himself, which comes to much the same as being circumcised, which means he must be a Jew. And evidently there is a link 'between the monastic homosexuality of *Parsifal*, centred around the leadership of an intuitively inspired youth, and the not dissimilar fellowship of Ernst Röhm's troopers. Not the *Ring* but *Parsifal* was the Wagner work whose mythology was powerful enough to leave an indelible mark on Germany' (Gutman).

Such views can't possibly be made to fit the drama in a

coherent way – they can't begin to. For one thing, Wagner had worked out the course of the drama in all essentials in 1865, before he embraced some of his later theories in an extreme form, or others at all. For another, the blood which is referred to in the drama is the Saviour's, and whatever may happen to it, racial pollution is not among the conceivable risks. If one studied and listened to the work itself with the greatest care, without knowing of Wagner's attitudes as expressed in his contemporaneous writings, it *could* never occur to one that it had any connection with anti-Semitic views. It may seem strange that someone could fervently advocate a set of convictions simultaneously with producing his most deeply-felt work of art, and that the second should have nothing to do with the first, but just that is what we find.

The second and much more plausible way in which *Parsifal* is regularly misinterpreted consists in seeing it as a religious, specifically a Christian, work. Why otherwise, both those who welcome and those who deplore what they take to be that fact ask, should Wagner have called it a stage-consecrating festival play? And if it is not a Christian work, as opposed to a work which is to a large extent about Christians (though remember that Christ is never referred to by name) and their failings and eventual salvation, what is the significance of the celebration of the Eucharist in Act I, the prayers which can hardly be addressed to anyone but the Christian God, the point of Parsifal's baptising Kundry and telling her to have faith in the Redeemer, and much else besides?

Yet who would have their Christian faith enhanced by *Parsifal*, or how could it effect a conversion? – two basic criteria for something's being a Christian work, surely. Of course the answer could be that Wagner's intention was to produce a Christian drama, in the most straightforward way, but that he failed and therefore the work is broken-backed. But here we have to return to our actual experience of it, which is, one or two brief passages apart, marvellously unified and coherent, and to remain true to that. The work is primarily about Parsifal's progress to enlightenment through compassion, and his subsequent ability to put the Hall of the Grail in order. That he manages to accomplish this without supernatural aid is clear; or if it isn't, recall that quotation from 'Art and Religion', about deploying beliefs as symbols. As long as Amfortas goes on crying to the All-Merciful, we have seen that he gets only a dusty answer. There is, correlatively, no point in Parsifal's development at which one could say that without the intervention of divine grace he would have remained powerless to accomplish his mission. Each stage is charted in psychological terms. Wagner's music, in this work at its most consistently subtle, economical and moving, enables us to feel with Parsifal and to live through his process of enlightenment. That is of the essence.

Even so, it might still be argued, what is it all in aid of if not the salvation of the Knighthood in general and Amfortas in particular? And how is that effected? Those are leading questions, for it does seem that the thrust of the work is that God helps those who help themselves, and quite notably doesn't help those who don't. But His presence *is* required to make sense of the process. How, otherwise, does Parsifal's compassion effect anything? Do such deeds as touching Amfortas's wound with the Spear heal, in a world which contains no supernatural agents or forces? Yes, if one takes these acts as symbols, though it is important to recall that Wagner is not only operating with a mixture of Christian and pagan symbols, but also that he was committed to Schopenhauer's philosophy of the primacy of the Will, more at this stage of his life than ever before. He was thus also still convinced of the pain inherent in being alive, and of the sovereign value of the identification of one's own sufferings with those of others. It is only in terms of this ethic of compassion, founded on a metaphysic of the unity of living things, that *Parsifal* makes sense. As soon as one has grasped that, the apparently Christian elements in the work, which can be embarrassing or seem merely added for colour, function much more actively as constituents in a profound drama of spiritual awakening and fulfilment. New life is brought to the Grail community, and it will be able to continue, invigorated, not through any injection of supernatural energy-boosters, but through the radiant example of Parsifal, showing the possibility of emerging triumphant from gruelling ordeals, neither complacent in his achievement nor exhausted by it.

I have said far too little about the music of *Parsifal*, admired enormously even by those who feel that it needs to be firmly separated from the repulsive drama. It certainly has a quality, in the outer acts, which has usually been compared to illumination from within, and also its vocabulary of pain seems to know no limits. What makes it so extraordinary is that it possesses these features simultaneously, and that leads me to a last tentative reflection on it. In the Prelude, the Transformation Music in Act I, Parsifal's central outburst in Act II, and throughout Act III, exaltation and desolation, pain and consolation, merge into one another in a way that reminds me of what Rilke wrote to a friend in 1923, apropos of his *Duino Elegies* and the *Sonnets to Orpheus*: 'Whoever does not, sometime or other, give his full consent, his full and joyous consent, to the dreadfulness of life, can never take possession of the unutterable abundance and power of our existence; can only walk on its edge, and one day, when the judgement is given, will have been neither alive nor dead. To show the identity of dreadfulness and bliss, these two faces on the same divine head, indeed this one single face, which just presents itself this way or that, according to our distance from it or the state of mind in which we perceive it.' If you think that that is outrageous mumbo-jumbo, you will almost certainly think the same about *Parsifal*. If you find it profound, it could well provide the most valuable brief commentary on Wagner's last work, and on a central theme which runs through them all.

15

Postlude:
Wagner and Culture

There can be no question, everyone will agree, that Wagner was trying to do some important things. I have tried to show what some of them were, and to trace a degree of unity through his works, of a kind which is often found in the greatest artists. But before I close I would like to press the matter a little further, since a deep understanding of Wagner is so easily avoided, thanks to the glamour of his surfaces. No one who has followed the argument thus far will deny that Wagner's preoccupations were those which can be traced in artists from Homer onwards, even if he uses all the resources of modernity, indeed was responsible for the creation of a good number of them. But a final emphatic claim about his abiding central concern, critically tactless as it may be, is also very much in his own spirit. It could also be thought that to advance a possibly surprising claim about what he meant is to be a faithful critic, since that was what he often did himself.

My claim, then, is this: Wagner makes repeated assaults, both in his discursive writings and in his dramatic works, on the most exasperating and obsessive of all issues: what, in our lives, are we prepared to accept as equivalent to the losses which are constantly inflicted upon us, most often by our-selves? He sees life as a continual attempt to make good what we either have been deprived of, or – what may come to the same thing – what we feel we have been deprived of. These deprivations may be of three kinds: those which we are responsible for, through negligence, recklessness, over-reaching, and so forth; those which we suffer at the hands of contingent but common circumstance, including especially the violations of other greedy agents; and those which are the inevitable consequence of being what and who we are, individuated beings in time, with a certain and swift end to all our efforts. We have to cope with ourselves, our environments, and the ineliminable conditions of existence and its termination. Whatever else, Wagner puts and maintains these obdurate facts at the forefront of all his art. That is, it seems to me, a necessary condition of being a very great artist, though of course it is not a sufficient one. Consciousness of our deepest problems may just as easily lead to portentous vacuity or metaphysical posturing as to genuinely serious attempts to cope with them. And it is the recurrent charge of anti-Wagnerians that his art is solemn and pretentious, possessing to a unique and therefore uniquely annoying degree all the trappings of depth, and wholly lacking the core which would justify them.

A decisive rebuttal of the charge is not possible, not one of the things that criticism can achieve, since criticism can only encourage and help people to articulate their responses; they have to judge for themselves the value of what has elicited those responses. So in this book I have tried to clear out of the way some of the more obvious and a few of the less obvious obstacles to understanding. I don't believe that it is possible to do anything valuable critically which is different in kind, though of course someone with more insight and sensitivity could do something better in degree. However, at this last stage I want to reiterate that Wagner unquestionably has his sights on the right targets, however misguided or perverse his handling of his weapon – his art – may be.

We have often noticed that Wagner is peculiarly absorbed by people who are intransigent, imperious in their demands on life, impatient with restrictions on their range of feeling and action, apparently unregarding of the claims of others, or willing to make exorbitant demands on others' capacity for sympathy and self-sacrifice. One question that his concern with such figures provokes is whether he is giving a mythic portrayal of what he regarded as a set of contemporary ills, or whether he thought that the characters he created were 'purely human', not to be located specifically in the culture of which he was a part. His prose writings are ambiguous on this score, and even if they weren't, they would not settle the matter conclusively for us. Perhaps it doesn't matter all that much: his message is for us, whether we regard ourselves as fundamentally akin to people of most times and places, or whether we take ourselves to be determined by our historical and geographical positioning. What is clear is that Wagner was intent on reanimating myth for modern man, an activity which might either give or restore to us a sense of our possible greatness, and one so fraught with difficulties that there is no need to rehearse them. Wagner, like Nietzsche, found intolerable the smallness of contemporary life, its preoccupation with matters which would obviously shrink our souls still further. His life's work is a continuous effort to show how we might gain or regain the dimensions of mystery and potentiality which are certainly missing in a secular age. To accomplish that he took the traditional patterns of tragedy, but repeatedly denied tragic conclusions. His mature works, with the exception, naturally, of *Die Meistersinger*, are pervaded by tragic feeling, but their resolutions suggest that whatever might be hurled at us, or undermine us from within, there is still to be discovered, or rediscovered, an heroic constituent in human nature which can take anything and manage to survive.

But is there? Is heroism a striving after something appallingly hard to attain, but still possible, or is it a gloriously doomed state of mind leading to gloriously doomed enterprises? Or is it a notion which we would do well to abolish, which indeed many people already succeed in doing without, and are all the better for it? That is a question not only for Wagner, but it certainly *is* one for him. We think of heroes in the first place as men capable of performing physical tasks of great daring, and though the connotations of the word 'hero' have now been so watered down that it means little more than the central figure of a work, in Wagner it retains much of its pristine force. That is both a strength and an embarrassment. For in our culture physical prowess is not much prized in serious circles, and certainly is not what we require in our most troublesome situations, as it was for the writers of the great epics and the Greek tragedies. Isn't a hero in that sense someone whom we can only take an interest in if we regard him as in some say symbolic? Or is Wagner trying to re-establish the primacy of the physical?

The answers to these, and other difficult and related questions, are complex. There is the whole issue of Wagner's relationship to culture, as we now understand it, we who live in advanced industrial societies. On the one hand we are individualists, keen on the establishment and maintenance of high profiles. On the other we accept that as members of extremely elaborately organised societies we have to behave according to many demanding codes of conduct, which constitute for us culture or civilisation. Wagner's characters share these twin responsibilities, but they are involved in culture at a far simpler though not necessarily less rigorous stage. A large area of Wagner's concern is how to reconcile the two: for him, most of the time, the demands of the individual self are absolute, and that is what creates the material of his dramas. Under what circumstances is it possible to live a completely fulfilled existence, giving rein to what, in the *Ring*, he calls love as opposed to law?

And it is in the *Ring* above all that we are confronted, time and again, with the question of equivalences, the question on which everything else turns. The *Ring* begins in a state of what seems like sempiternal entropy, in which, so the Prelude and the initial gambollings of the Rhinemaidens suggest, nothing will ever change or ever need to. It takes Alberich, who expresses elemental desire in a curiously unattractive form, to alter the cosmic economy, or rather to show that it is an illusion: there is need, want, lack (Wagner's all-purpose term is '*Noth*') in the world, and that shows that it has departed from, or not reached, stability. Shockingly, Alberich is prepared to forgo possession of another's body for domination of the world: or that is what at first seems to be the case. But we soon discover that there is a world elsewhere, one in which Light-Alberich, as Wotan is bemusingly called (though it is a piece of nomenclature fraught with significances which Wagner, worried about the already large conceptual element in the work, mainly suppressed), has already engaged in a primal act of exchange. He has forfeited one eye – part of his capacity for experiencing the world directly – for knowledge, the capacity to understand and thus to control. That we are not vouchsafed this information until a very late stage in the cycle is a teasing part of Wagner's strategy for getting us to realise the eternal and recurring nature of the issues which he is presenting to us. Wotan and Alberich are thus on a collision course, one which can never be resolved unless the terms of their conflict are radically changed by a new type of being: one who loves. But what concept of love can we evolve which will not give rise to a rebirth of the same conflict? Can there be a love which is not a matter of possession, even if the possession is mutual? Wagner always insisted that the fundamental kind of love is sexual, and that all other varieties are founded on that, in some way. The category of desire is his basic one, which is no doubt the ultimate reason why he found Schopenhauer so congenial and liberating. For Schopenhauer is the first philosopher to make our contact with the world primarily a matter of will, rather than of perception or reason. His pessimism, which for him flowed immediately from that, requires the added premise that we can never satisfy our desires, and was something which Wagner both accepted but also, with the boundless optimism of the artist, for whom art can effect miracles, was determined to overcome.

Schopenhauer, too, had been determined to evade it, at severe cost of consistency. And, more worryingly still, his ways of evading it turn out to be all too conventional: morality, disinterested pursuit of knowledge and beauty, and most dubiously of all, the denial of the will by the will. He is thus, apart from the last of these, where he retreats into a kind of nihilistic mysticism, a reactionary. Wagner, a very idiosyncratic disciple, the only kind he could be of anyone or anything, took Schopenhauer more seriously than the philosopher took himself. Wagner went on to question whether the agonies of desire, of willing, couldn't be dealt with by a whole new way of living, one in which people – individual manifestations of the World Will – might find fulfilment rather than a kind of compromised respite. And if they could, what would be the consequences for their relationships with the rest of the world, human and non-human?

Put in such dauntingly general terms, the question, and the ambition which gives rise to it, sound hopeless. Wagner needed to see his works in the most portentous way possible, in order to gain the energy to compose them. That is a major reason for the obscurity and vagueness of his prose writings. But then the dramas themselves seem to deal with such 'interesting' specimens that it becomes hard to see them as exemplary. And yet the violence of the reactions which his art elicits, and which one always has to return to, does suggest that he is striking at something in us which works at a level where we are uneasy: uneasy, that is, about investigations which take place into it.

But if all the greatest art concerns itself with issues of such profundity, as I think it must, why is it that this art in particular occasions such anxiety, or if you prefer, disgust, or ecstasy? That is the first and the final question. The answer has something to do with Wagner's remorseless insistence on our attempting to cope with the matter of equivalences. It is deeply embarrassing to be asked so insistently what we count as most valuable, in other words what we are prepared to sacrifice in order to feel fulfilled. For we can only give a truthful reply by examining how much we care about our own satisfactions at the cost of other people's. The notorious self-centredness of Wagner's characters (not to mention his own) is most comfortably coped with by dismissing them as fantasies, hardly to be counted as members of a conceivably civilised society. We know that in order to co-exist we have to suppress much of what we would most like to express, and hardly want the issue reopened at this stage.

But that is exactly Wagner's point. His art is devoted to refusing to accept that the decisions we have made in order to be civilised were the right ones. In this he is, of course, at one with the Nietzsche of *The Genealogy of Morals* and the other late, disturbing masterpieces which he produced in the five years following Wagner's death. Nietzsche mourned Wagner creatively by working out his own answers to the questions which, in his opinion, Wagner had botched. It is therefore not surprising that these two one-time allies and friends elicit such similar responses, and have been misappropriated in such uncannily similar ways. Not that they reach the same conclusions; but they affect us in a comparable manner, calling into question the very terms in which we feel it is necessary, or even possible, to have a debate. Nietzsche undermines us by his extraordinary conceptual juxtapositions, forcing us, by the invention of myths of masters and slaves, to see ourselves as the outcome of a disastrous process which he alleges is historical. And yet, despite the evident absence of hard data to support his claims, his depiction of the sterility of our lives is so compelling that we accept him in a way which we would normally reserve for the communications of a consummate artist. Wagner is a consummate artist, but often seems to impel us to talk about him as though he were a philosopher. In the best writing about both of them, the barrier between philosophy and art is overcome, or discarded. It is a gesture of despair to say that what really matters about Wagner is his music, or a frivolous refusal – they come to the same thing – to take him seriously.

For Wagner was right, however varying his formulations on the subject, when he claimed that his music was written in the service of something else. It is one of the ironies of artistic history that he inspired, as no other person ever has, various movements which can be called 'Art for art's sake'. Because he wanted his art to accomplish so much, he invested it with a power which makes it seem an end in itself. Time and again, as one listens to – supposing one has given up seeing – Wagner's works, one finds oneself so captivated by his means of expression that one hardly retains the capacity for apprehending. What Wagner intended to be transparent possesses a glorious opacity. Even so, there are distinctions to be made. For many people the gorgeous fabric of Wagner's music, perhaps even his music-drama, is an object of contemplation in itself. But it is also possible, while being saturated by it, to have one's vision of things transformed, at any rate for a time. The world can seem to be different, and not in a merely metaphysically fairy-tale way. One can be led to interrogate the categories by which one normally experiences, and to ponder those vexing questions about what matters most – what one would exchange for what, to be brutal – in a way that otherwise only Shakespeare effects. Nietzsche tells us, imperiously and irresistibly, to think about the basis of our evaluations, about our whole set of moral attitudes. Wagner may be more dangerous (Nietzsche certainly thought he was, and envied him for it) in making us feel what it would be like to live with a radically different set of values. Of course it is extremely unlikely that we shall, just as it is extremely unlikely that even the most receptive reader of the Sermon on the Mount will give away all his possessions. The inertia of culture is immense, and when we meditate on the price we would pay, especially perhaps the price we would pay in our relations with the persons who matter most to us, we are overcome and decide that discretion is the wiser course.

And even if we didn't come to that conclusion, how would we begin to change our lives, where would the change start? To say it would begin by taking hard thought sounds pretty pathetic, though it is partly right. If it strikes one as absurd, it is because Wagner employs means which seem appropriate for a conversion, and it is not characteristic of converts to think. Whatever or whoever it is that converts them, they recognise an authority which has an immediate transforming effect on their whole life. But maybe we should acknowledge the possibility of another kind of conversion, one which I believe is not all that uncommon, though since it lacks the sensational qualities usually associated with conversions it can easily be overlooked. There is also the complication that what is gradual is thereby much less readily recognised, except by someone who has not encountered the convert concerned for a long time. And it is typical, too, for at least very many people who are dissatisfied with the level of their life, to want it to alter not only drastically, but instantly. Though it is fairly widely agreed that love at first sight is exciting but hardly something to bank on, there are many other experiences which it is hoped will be not only immediate in their impact, but long-lasting; but they seem to me to be in much the same position as love.

It might seem that Wagner's art, being so immediate, if not rude, in its impact, is a particularly implausible candidate as something to live with and slowly be affected by. Certainly Wagnerians do tend to be aesthetically born-again types, who vividly recall the occasion on which they had their first authentic encounter with the Master. And the vast majority of what is written about him suggests that the authors either have gone no further than their initial experience, or have chosen, or needed, to displace it by endless discussions of one or another aspect of the life and work which are, in the end, quite pointless. To live with Wagner's art without its becoming simply a ritual or alternatively a subject for musicological, etc. investigations, is, to judge from the printed reports, very difficult. I have done my best, for the moment, to show that it is possible, I hope without a smothering surfeit of self-consciousness.

For those of us who have a temperamental disposition to think about the issues of our lives in terms which are in large part provided for us by great art, it may well be a matter of chance which artist or artists one encounters at which state of one's life, and thus of whom one cares most about. Some artists are, for anyone who has a traditional education, inescapable, liable therefore to become fixtures and to run the risk of turning into the wallpaper of our lives. Shakespeare is the obvious case, and it is important that styles of criticism of him should change so that he becomes once more a foreground figure. Even such deformations of criticism as the New Historicism or Cultural Materialism have their part to play in giving rise to indignant refutations, since by their sometimes plausible absurdities they provoke us to reanimate our responses.

Wagner neither has, nor is ever likely to have, that status. It would be an alarming world in which he achieved it. Recently a German said to me, 'You English have your Shakespeare; we have our Wagner.' Granted my passion for Wagner and my lack of cultural chauvinism it was perhaps odd that I was so shocked by her remark. I didn't want to say, 'But Shakespeare is greater than Wagner.' But I did feel a strong urge to protest about Wagner's being seen as a part of the cultural landscape in the way that Shakespeare is (even for Germans, thanks to Tieck and Schlegel). Each of them raises issues which we have to dwell on, and provides us with many of the concepts for discussion. But in Shakespeare there is always a framework, but not a frame, which is why he is often alleged to have no views, except for the view that we need to interrogate our experiences with vigour and pertinacity. Wagner, by sharpest contrast, has a set of attitudes which may be hard to work out, and which undoubtedly vary from work to work. He reaches, not so much irritably as furiously, after certainties, and per-suades us that he has reached them, though we may feel that there is something odd about a state of mind which has the feeling of certainty without a clear content.

Finally, but by no means conclusively: think of the charac-teristic way in which Shakespeare's plays open and close. They are almost weirdly unassertive in their first scenes, and though that may be part of his consummate artistry, it does mean that one wills one's way into attending to them. And their endings are notoriously of the 'Take him up and bear him hence' manner, seeming to concede that anything in the nature of a firm declaration of completion would be a betrayal. Wagner is never more impressive than in his commencements, which have all the force of an important theorem to be proved. And the works give their audiences a uniquely gratifying sense of fulfilment by ending – with, as I have shown, the signal exception of *Parsifal* – with a massive musico-dramatic QED. For anyone writing a book about Wagner, it would be unwise to follow his example. There is always much more to be said.

CHRONOLOGY

1813 22 May: Wilhelm Richard Wagner (henceforth RW) born in Leipzig, ninth child of Carl Friedrich Wilhelm Wagner, police actuary, and Johanna Pätz. 16 August: baptised in Thomaskirche. 23 November: father dies of typhus, a month after the 'Battle of the Nations'.

1814 28 August: Johanna Wagner marries the painter and actor Ludwig Geyer, long-time friend of the family. RW often believed himself to be Geyer's son, and thought also that Geyer may have been a Jew. Family moves to Dresden.

1821 30 September: Geyer dies. October: Geyer's younger brother Carl takes RW into his care.

1822 December: RW becomes a pupil in the Dresden Kreuzschule; he begins piano lessons. He hears and is excited by Weber's *Der Freischütz*.

1826 RW studies Greek enthusiastically, begins to write an epic poem (lost).

1827 RW confirmed, under name 'Geyer', in Dresden. Moves to Leipzig.

1828 January: RW a pupil in Nicolaischule in Leipzig. He writes a verse tragedy, takes composition lessons. Autumn: begins to study harmony. Greatly impressed by Mozart and Beethoven.

1829 April: RW hears the great soprano Wilhelmine Schröder-Devrient (he later claims as Leonore in Beethoven's *Fidelio*, but that is part of his 'mythological' autobiography); she makes a profound impression on him, more by her dramatic ability than her voice. RW's first compositions: two piano sonatas, string quartet, etc.

1830 RW arranges Beethoven's Ninth Symphony for piano; composes orchestral overtures. 24 December: performance of his Overture in B major in Leipzig.

1831 RW composes *Seven Pieces for Goethe's 'Faust'*. February: leaves school without certificate, registers at Leipzig University as music student. Autumn: RW registers as composition student of Theodor Weinlig, cantor of Thomaskirche. Several compositions, mostly for piano.

1832 RW composes sonatas, overtures, etc., concludes study with Weinlig and writes his Symphony in C major. Autumn: begins composition of his first opera, *Die Hochzeit* (The Wedding), to his own text. He soon abandons it.

1833 RW writes the text of his first complete opera *Die Feen* (The Fairies), after a play by Gozzi. February: goes to Würzburg for his first post, under his brother Albert, as choir-master. Begins composition of *Die Feen*.

1834 January: RW completes composition of *Die Feen*. June: publishes his first article, 'German Opera'. June: writes prose sketch for *Das Liebesverbot* (The Ban on Love). Summer: becomes acquainted with the actress Minna Planer. October: becomes music director of Magdeburg Theatre.

1835 January: RW begins composition of *Das Liebesverbot*. Summer: travels to Bohemia and Bavaria to engage singers.

1836 RW completes score of *Das Liebesverbot*. 21 March: first performance, disastrous; there is not a second one during RW's lifetime. 24 November: marries Minna Planer in Königsberg.

1837 April: RW music director of Königsberg Theatre. 31 May: Minna secretly disappears with a lover to Dresden. RW pursues her, she leaves him again and only returns in October. July: writes prose sketch of opera *Rienzi* based on Bulwer Lytton's novel. Becomes music director in Riga.

1838 August: RW begins composing *Rienzi*. 15 November: launches a new concert series, in which he conducts Beethoven Symphonies 3–8, works by Mozart, Weber, Cherubini, Mendelssohn and himself.

1839 July: RW leaves Riga with idea of making his fortune in Paris with *Rienzi*. Minna has a miscarriage. Terrible sea voyage from Pillau to London, lasting three weeks. Stays in Old Compton Street. 20

August: to Boulogne, where RW meets Meyerbeer. September: travels to Paris, with recommendations from Meyerbeer, but makes no professional headway. Composes songs, some in French.

1840 RW at his wits' end in Paris, arranging popular operas for flute and piano, etc. to survive. Writes first version of *A Faust Overture*. Prose-sketch of *Der fliegende Holländer*. Meets Liszt for first time. 12 July: begins a series of articles on musical life for *Revue et Gazette musicale*. November: finishes score of *Rienzi*.

1841 The French hell continues. 29 April: RW moves to Meudon, suburb of Paris. 2 July: sells libretto of *Der fliegende Holländer*.

1842 7 April: RW leaves Paris, his hopes all unfulfilled. 20 October: first performance of *Rienzi*, with Schröder-Devrient as Adriano. It is a huge success.

1843 January: first performance of *Der fliegende Holländer*, with Schröder-Devrient as Senta; another, though less striking, success. RW writes sketch of Tannhäuser. May–June: RW composes *Das Liebesmahl der Apostel* (The Love-Feast of the Apostles), a choral work, performed in church in July. RW reads Grimm's *German Mythology*, begins composing *Tannhäuser*. October: new house in Dresden, RW begins to collect his library of works on German myth and a wide variety of medieval subjects.

1844 January: RW travels to Berlin, conducts *Der fliegende Holländer* there. Meets Mendelssohn. Arranges for Weber's remains to be moved from London to Dresden, writes music for the reinterment, makes a speech at the grave (December).

1845 RW completes *Tannhäuser*. July: prose sketches of *Die Meistersinger von Nürnberg* and *Lohengrin*. 19 October: first performance of *Tannhäuser* in Dresden.

1846 5 April: RW conducts for the first time Beethoven's Ninth Symphony in Dresden, setting new standards of orchestral performance and symphonic interpretation. Works on *Lohengrin*. December: RW works on his revision of Gluck's *Iphigénie in Aulis*.

1847 22 February: first performance of revision of *Iphigénie in Aulis*. October: first Berlin performance of *Rienzi*, under RW.

1848 9 January: RW's mother dies in Leipzig. March: RW conducts his own version of Palestrina's Stabat Mater in Dresden. 28 April: finishes *Lohengrin*. April/May: RW draws up plans for reformation of Dresden's musical life, gives address on republicanism and monarchy. Meets and becomes friend of Russian anarchist Mikhail Bakhunin. July: travels to Vienna, meets Grillparzer and the critic Hanslick, later to be parodied as Beckmesser. Writes *The Nibelungen. World History from the Saga*. Autumn: writes anonymous article for republican journal. Text of 'Siegfried's Tod' (Siegfried's Death).

1849 Sketch for drama 'Jesus of Nazareth'. Further anonymous articles in favour of revolution. May: revolution in Dresden, RW taking active part. The uprising is quelled, and RW narrowly escapes arrest, a price is put on his head, and he escapes to Zurich. End of July: *Art and Revolution*. September: Minna follows to Zurich. *The Art-Work of the Future*

1850 1 January: RW gives first of many concerts of Beethoven's and his own works in Zurich. Sketch of an opera 'Wieland der Schmied' (Wieland the Smith). Travels to Paris. March/May: affair with Jessie Laussot in Bordeaux. July: returns to Zurich. August: musical sketches for 'Siegfried's Tod'. First performance of *Lohengrin* in Weimar under Liszt, Wagner sits in Lucerne 'following' the performance, watch in hand. Writes *Judaism in Music*. October: Hans von Bülow becomes a pupil. RW begins *Opera and Drama* (completed 1851).

1851 Text of 'Der junge Siegfried' (Young Siegfried), later simply *Siegfried*. July–August: *A Communication to my Friends*. Autumn: Julie Ritter arranges regular payments to RW, until 1859.

1852 RW meets the rich merchant Otto Wesendonck and his wife Mathilde. New ending for 'Siegfried's Tod' inspired by reading Feuerbach.

1853 Private printing of *Der Ring des Nibelungen* (text). February: RW reads the *Ring* to friends in Hotel Baur. June: RW composes sonata for Mathilde Wesendonck. July: travels with Liszt and Georg Herwegh. September: conceives the Prelude to *Das Rheingold* (RW's account in his autobiography is another piece of mild mythology). October: travels to Berlin and meets Liszt's daughter Cosima. 1 November: begins composition of *Das Rheingold*.

1854 RW begins composition of *Die Walküre*. Falls in love with Mathilde Wesendonck. Georg Herwegh introduces RW to Schopenhauer's *The World as Will and Representation*, which he immediately reads several times. First thoughts of *Tristan und Isolde*.

1855 RW revises *A Faust Overture*. March–June: conducts eight concerts in London; received by Queen Victoria. Meets and becomes friends with Berlioz.

1856 Gets to know Gottfried Keller. Finishes score of *Die Walküre*. May: sketch of an opera, 'Die Sieger' (The Victors), on a Buddhist subject. June–August: drastic water cure. Changes end of *Götterdämmerung* text to accord with Schopenhauerian views. September: begins composing *Siegfried*. December: first musical sketches of *Tristan und Isolde*.

1857 Writes essay 'On Franz Liszt's Symphonic Poems'. 28 April: moves into Asyl with Minna, house provided by Otto Wesendonck adjacent to his villa. May: first ideas for *Parsifal*. August: breaks off composition of *Siegfried*. Text of *Tristan und Isolde*. October: begins to compose *Tristan*. 30 November: begins setting five poems of Mathilde Wesendonck for voice and piano, two subtitled 'Sketch for *Tristan*. 31 December: finishes composition sketch of Act I of *Tristan*, with effusive poem of dedication to Mathilde.

1858 Increasing conflicts with Minna over his relationship with Mathilde. 14 January: travels to Paris, where Berlioz reads him the text of *Les Troyens*; RW not impressed. April: Minna intercepts a letter from RW to Mathilde, violent scene follows. August: RW abandons the Asyl, travels via Geneva to Venice, where in solitude he continues to compose *Tristan*, Act II.

1859 RW finishes Act II of *Tristan*, moves to Lucerne and completes Act III in August. September: RW reunited with Minna in Paris.

1860 January/February: RW conducts concerts in Paris. July: partial amnesty granted. September: rehearsals commence in Paris for *Tannhäuser* in a new version. RW revises the Venusberg ballet entirely.

1861 March: new production of *Tannhäuser* ends in enormous scandal, thanks to Jockey Club. RW withdraws it after third performance. May: RW sees *Lohengrin* for the first time in Vienna. During the year RW develops his ideas on *Die Meistersinger*, and works out most of the overture on a train journey in November.

1862 January: poem of *Die Meistersinger*. February: rents a house in Biebrich on the Rhine, is joined by Minna, and they spend 'ten days in hell'. March: beginnings of relationships with Mathilde Maier and Friederike Meyer. Full amnesty. July: Hans von Bülow and his wife Cosima Liszt visit RW in Biebrich. September: RW conducts *Lohengrin* for the first time, in Frankfurt. November: RW conducts overture to *Die Meistersinger* for the first time (Leipzig). Sees Minna for the last time, Dresden. Travels to Vienna with Friederike Meyer. Reads *Die Meistersinger* to an audience which includes Hanslick, who to RW's surprise takes offence.

1863 January: concerts in Vienna. February: RW travels to Prague, Berlin, St Petersburg. March/April: concerts in St Petersburg and Moscow. RW takes up residence in Penzing near Vienna. November: RW meets Turgenev, he and Cosima vow eternal love.

1864 The eighteen-year-old Ludwig II becomes King of Bavaria. RW flees Vienna on account of his debts. 4 May: RW in hiding in Stuttgart, found by Ludwig's secretary Pfistermeister, who tells him Ludwig wants to settle all his debts and establish him in a house near Munich. June: Cosima comes with her two daughters for a long visit. August: *Homage March* for Ludwig. Liszt visits. October: RW moves to house in Munich. Ludwig plans a theatre for performance of RW's works in Munich. RW begins full score of Act II of *Siegfried*.

1865 February: first anonymous attacks on RW in Munich press. 10 April: Isolde, first child of RW and Cosima, born. On same day rehearsals of *Tristan* begin under Bülow. 10 June: first performance of *Tristan*. July: RW begins dictation of his biography *Mein Leben* to Cosima. His first Tristan, Ludwig Schnorr von Carolsfeld, dies. August: first prose sketch of *Parsifal*. December: public opinion forces RW to leave Munich. He rents a house in Geneva.

1866 25 January; Minna dies in Dresden. March: Cosima comes to Geneva. April: RW settles in Haus Tribschen on Lake Lucerne, for the eight happiest years of his life. May: Cosima joins him with her daughters. October: Hans Richter begins working as RW's secretary and copyist.

1867 17 February: Eva, RW's and Cosima's second child, born. 24 October: RW completes score of *Die Meistersinger*.

1868 21 July: first performance of *Die Meistersinger*, in Munich; RW sits in the King's box with him. Conductor: Bülow. September–October: Cosima tells Bülow she wants to marry RW. RW explains his relationship with her to Ludwig. November: RW meets Friedrich Nietzsche for the first time, in Leipzig.

1869 RW finishes Act II of *Siegfried*. New edition of *Judaism in Music*. May: Nietzsche visits RW in Tribschen for the first time; 22 further visits follow until 1872, a very close relationship. 6 June: RW's and Cosima's son Siegfried born. 22 September: against RW's wishes, first performance of *Das Rheingold* in Munich, commanded by Ludwig. October: *On Conducting*. December: RW reads *Parsifal* to Cosima and Nietzsche.

1870 First ideas of performing *Ring* in Bayreuth. 26 July: against RW's wishes, first performance of *Die Walküre* in Munich. 25 August: RW marries Cosima in Protestant church in Lucerne. 25 December: first performance of *Siegfried Idyll*, composed secretly, takes place in Tribschen.

1871 February: RW completes *Siegfried*. *Kaisermarsch*. 16 April: RW and Cosima pay first visit to Bayreuth. RW decides to build a theatre there. May: RW received by Bismarck. November: first arrangements with Bayreuth town council for land for theatre.

1872 January: Nietzsche sends RW *The Birth of Tragedy*, RW very impressed. April: RW leaves Tribschen. 22 May: RW lays foundation stone of Festspielhaus, conducts Beethoven's Ninth Symphony in the existing opera house. November: RW and Cosima begin touring Germany looking for singers for the *Ring*.

1873 Further extensive preparations for first festival. September: Bruckner visits RW in Bayreuth, dedicates his Third Symphony to him. December: RW completes Act I of *Götterdämmerung*.

1874 Ludwig makes large loan for Festspielhaus. 28 April: RW and family move into Haus Wahnfried ('Freedom from Illusion'), their Bayreuth home. 26 June: RW completes Act II of *Götterdämmerung*, begins first rehearsals for *Ring*. 21 November: RW completes *Götterdämmerung*, twenty-six years after first thoughts on subject.

1875 March: two concerts in Vienna. Throughout year further travels and rehearsals.

1876 March: *American Centennial March*. 15 August: first cycle of *Ring* begins in Festspielhaus, attended by Kaiser Wilhelm I, Emperor Dom Pedro II of Brazil, high society of Europe, innumerable composers; Nietzsche attends first cycle, flees, for assorted reasons. RW bitterly disappointed with performances: 'I wish I were dead' to Cosima. September–December: travels in Italy, last meeting with Nietzsche, in Sorrento. Huge deficit from festival.

1877 19 April: RW finishes text of *Parsifal*. May: RW and Richter give series of concerts in London's Albert Hall to pay off deficit; artistic success, financial failure. The Wagners become friendly with George Eliot, Burne-Jones, etc. Received by Queen Victoria at Windsor. September: RW begins composing *Parsifal*.

1878 January: first number of *Bayreuther Blätter* appears, house journal of the Wagner cult, continuing until 1938. 26 December: RW conducts first performance of *Parsifal* Prelude in Wahnfried.

1879 Work on *Parsifal*. December: the Wagner family travel to Italy. Increasing ill-health.

1880 January–August: RW and family in Naples. RW occupied with writings about religion and art, etc. November: RW and Ludwig meet for the last time.

1881 25 April: RW finishes score of Act I of *Parsifal*. May: RW attends *Ring* in Berlin. Visited by racial theorist Count Gobineau, whom he much admires, in Bayreuth. 20 October: RW finishes Act II of *Parsifal*. November: the Wagners go to Palermo, stay in the Hôtel des Palmes.

1882 January: RW finishes *Parsifal*. Renoir paints him. April: travels through Italy and Munich back to Bayreuth. 26 July: first performance of *Parsifal*, conducted by Hermann Levi. Sixteen performances in all, the last forty minutes of the final one conducted by RW, by now very ill, suffering from frequent heart attacks. September: RW and family travel to Venice, stay on Grand Canal in Palazzo Vendramin Calergi. November: Liszt visits and stays until January. 24 December: RW conducts his early symphony in the Teatro la Fenice.

1883 Hermann Levi comes to discuss the next festival. 13 February: RW has severe heart attack, dies in Cosima's arms. 18 February: RW buried in garden of Wahnfried.

SELECT BIBLIOGRAPHY

It is routinely claimed that there are more books on Wagner than on anyone who has ever lived, except for Jesus Christ and Napoleon. That is certainly false, but there is nonetheless a prodigious number, and the flow continues. I shall give a very short list, since anyone interested enough to read the books on it will then be in a position to make their own choice.

First a bit about Wagner's own writings. As I pointed out in the text, though they are often illuminating they are also verbose and frequently obscure. That is the case in the original, and is only compounded by the English version of the complete Prose Works (more or less), at present being reprinted in paperback. This translation, made by the bizarre William Ashton Ellis, is into a language only remotely related to English as anyone else knows it. But the task of translation has proved sufficiently daunting, or uncommercial, for no replacements of most of Ellis's work to have been attempted.

By far the most enjoyable and profitable way to acquaint oneself with Wagner's thinking is to read the Letters, in which he often expounds his thoughts both clearly and forcefully, and with a charm and wit almost always lacking in his formal prose. There is a superb *Selected Letters of Richard Wagner* translated and edited by Stewart Spencer and Barry Millington, with five hundred letters translated in whole or part, and very useful introductions to the six stages of Wagner's life into which they are divided. Many thousands of Wagner's letters survive, but many of the most significant for an understanding of his dramas are to be found in this large, compulsively readable volume.

Wagner's early journalism, strongly influenced in manner by Hoffmann, is selected in the delightful *Wagner Writes from Paris . . .* , translated by Robert Jacobs and Geoffrey Skelton. The latter is responsible for the complete translation of Cosima's *Diaries*, two vast volumes which record many of Wagner's remarks, as well as his day-to-day existence, for the last fourteen years of his life. Robert Jacobs, in *Three Wagner Essays*, produces a slightly abridged version of *On Conducting*, Wagner at his most incisive and authoritative, producing the most influential piece ever written on the subject. But for the great theoretical tracts, above all *Opera and Drama* and *A Communication to my Friends*, it looks as if we shall await new translations in vain.

The most useful and readable guide to the music dramas themselves remains Ernest Newman's *Wagner Nights*, alternatively *The Wagner Operas* (in the USA). Newman devotes a lavish amount of space to each work, first of all tracing the process by which it was written; then giving a detailed account of the plot, with lengthy quotations in English and many musical examples. He does not go in for interpretation, but he does sort out some of the tangles in the works. Some of his research is inevitably dated, but not seriously so. Given the usual misery of reading opera plots, it is an astonishingly enjoyable book. Briefer plot summaries can be found in *The Viking Opera Guide*, edited by Amanda Holden, Nicholas Kenyon and Stephen Walsh; together with largely reliable recommendations for recordings.

Interpretations of the dramas are naturally copious and often very idiosyncratic. They tend, nowadays, to divide into the *how* and the *what*. The great German musicologist Carl Dahlhaus, in his *Richard Wagner's Music Dramas*, gives perhaps the most succinct and helpful account of the specific dramatic and musical features of each work, while largely abstaining from giving his view of their import, or from passing any judgements. By contrast, Robert Raphael, in his *Richard Wagner*, is entirely concerned to elucidate their significance, and mainly does so very well, though often one feels he could be writing about spoken dramas. Deryck Cooke, in his unfinished *I Saw the World End*, gives an extremely detailed account of the *Ring*'s sources in Nordic myth, and provides his interpretation for the first two of the *Ring* dramas, often illuminatingly, sometimes naïvely. The English National Opera has published a short, cheap book on each of the dramas, with the complete text in German and English, many photographs of productions, and essays on aspects of the works which are of the highest interest. For anyone except the specialist, they will be enough, and are extraordinarily good value.

Wagner's life has been written many times, but new material is always coming to light, allegedly justifying yet another biography. The most exhaustive and satisfactory remains, once more, Ernest Newman's *The Life of Richard Wagner*, in four volumes. Immense as it is, it is hypnotically compelling. Newman began it in the early thirties and concluded it in the mid-forties, so it is in some respects, again, out of date. But it provides an unrivalled account of what that amazing life was like, and is balanced to a degree which few biographers manage. More brief, and more up-to-date, is Derek Watson's *Richard Wagner*. Curt von Westernhagen's *Wagner* is a work of piety by an old Wagnerian, selectively making use of modern research. He is scandalously silent on Wagner's anti-Semitism, but frank otherwise, and fascinatingly detailed. Geoffrey Skelton, in *Richard and Cosima Wagner*, gives a quite exceptionally well-written and comprehensive 'biography of a marriage'.

Wagner's impact on music and in general – what is currently called 'Wagner reception' – is comprehensively but compactly dealt with by a team of experts in *Wagnerism in European Culture and Politics*, edited by David C. Large and William Weber. The cataclysmic effect of *Tristan* on musicians, poets, novelists, etc. is dealt with in a pioneering piece of intellectual history: *The First Hundred Years of Wagner's Tristan*, by the hostile Elliott Zuckermann. As I remarked in the body of the text, there is a steady stream of books offering to demonstrate that all Wagner's villains are 'really' Jews, of which I shall not give details. Perhaps belonging to 'reception' too is the absorbing, candid and strikingly balanced *A History of the Bayreuth Festival* by Frederic Spotts.

Indispensable classic reactions to Wagner are Nietzsche's *The Case of Wagner* and *Nietzsche Contra Wagner*; his early pro-Wagner essay, *Richard Wagner in Bayreuth*, is not interesting, but is in his *Untimely Meditations*. Thomas Mann, who maintained an equivocal attitude, but found Wagner's art irresistible, wrote about him often, and his essays, letters, etc. on the subject are collected in *Pro and Contra Wagner*; the great 'The Sorrows and Grandeur of Richard Wagner' is the major essay, overflowing with insights. Theodor Adorno's *In Search of Wagner* is important because of its author, showing how a thinker of genius can be led by reacting to Wagner's art into wild postures of rejection, and sneaking admiration.

Wagner Handbook, edited by Ulrich Müller and Peter Wapnewski, translation edited by John Deathridge, is compendious to a degree. Whether you want to know about Wagner in Literature and Film, Wagner's Middle Ages, the Operas as Literary Works, or to consult a large bibliography, or read on any of the central areas in Wagner 'research', you will find at least one substantial chapter here.

INDEX

NOTE: Richard Wagner is abbreviated to RW.

227

Index

Index